BIBLIOTHECA IAGELLONICA. FONTES ET STUDIA
T. 19

THE AESTHETICS OF SENECAN TRAGEDY

BIBLIOTHECA IAGELLONICA. FONTES ET STUDIA

T. 19

Joanna Pypłacz

THE AESTHETICS OF SENECAN TRAGEDY

KRAKÓW 2010

Redaktor serii: Zdzisław Pietrzyk

Komitet redakcyjny
Monika Jaglarz, Andrzej Obrębski, Zdzisław Pietrzyk

Redakcja: Karolina Farrel
Korekta: Ewa Popielarz
Projekt okładki: Paweł Sepielak
Skład: Małgorzata Manterys-Rachwał

© Copyright by Joanna Pypłacz, Biblioteka Jagiellońska
and Księgarnia Akademicka Sp. z o.o., Kraków 2009

Na okładce wykorzystano obraz Henry'ego Fuseli'ego
pt. *Lady Macbeth seizing the daggers*

Cover illustration: *Lady Macbeth seizing the daggers* by Henry Fuseli
(reproduced by kind permission of the Tate Gallery, London)

ISBN 978-83-7638-017-9
ISSN 1425-851X

Książka została dofinansowana przez Uniwersytet Jagielloński

BIBLIOTEKA JAGIELLOŃSKA
Al. Mickiewicza 22
30-059 Kraków
www.bj.uj.edu.pl

Wydawca:
KSIĘGARNIA AKADEMICKA
30-008 Kraków, ul. św. Anny 6
Zamówienia przez księgarnię internetową:
www.akademicka.pl

A Raúl, el amor de mi vida

*An artist is an artist only by dint of his exquisite sense of Beauty —
a sense affording him rapturous enjoyment, but at the same time implying,
or involving, an equally exquisite sense of Deformity or disproportion.*

Edgar Allan Poe, *Fifty Suggestions*, "Graham's Magazine", 1849, V

Table of Contents

Introduction 9

Chapter I
An Imaginary Scene — Crossing the Frontier of Genre 15

Chapter II
Seneca and the Epic Poets 29

Chapter III
Contrariis in contraria agitur. The Contrast Technique 61

Chapter IV
The Aesthetics of Disgust 75

Chapter V
Musa Crudelis. The Birth of a New Aesthetic 93

Conclusion 115

Bibiliography 117

Introduction

As its title suggests, the present study is concerned with aesthetic issues that arise from a reading of the tragedies of Seneca the Younger. It will entail not only a close examination of the structure and texture of the tragedies, but also an investigation of their relationship to the works of earlier Roman poets — Virgil and Ovid in particular — the latter of whom, as Reiner Jakobi has shown,[1] Seneca used to imitate.

It is clear that Seneca's plays belong to the dramatic genre, but they differ greatly from all preceding drama. We do not know with any certainty what the purpose of these plays was and cannot give a definite answer to the vexed question of their possible performance on any kind of stage.[2]

Although many scholars suppose,[3] and others are convinced that Seneca's tragedies were indeed written for the stage,[4] it is obvious that these plays are highly descriptive and that many parts of them would be extremely difficult to stage in any "normal" theatre.[5] There is also written evidence to suggest that what the dramatists of the early Empire had in mind was not a normal play, but an oral recital[6] — which, of course, was also a kind of performance.[7]

---

[1] Cf. R. Jakobi, *Der Einfluß Ovids auf den Tragiker Seneca*, Berlin 1988; cf. G. W. M. Harrison, *"Semper ego auditor tantum?" Performance and physical setting of Seneca's plays*, [in:] *Seneca in Performance*, ed. by G. W. M. Harrison, London 2000, pp. 137-149.

[2] Cf. Seneca, *Medea*, transl. and introd. by F. Ahl, New York 1986, p. 18; cf. E. Wesołowska, *Postaci w "Medei" i "Fedrze" Seneki*, Poznań 1991, p. 7.

[3] Cf. L. Hermann, *Le Théâtre de Sénèque*, Paris 1924, pp. 153-232.

[4] Cf. D. Ferrin Sutton, *Seneca on the Stage*, Leiden 1986, p. 2; cf. G. W. M. Harrison, *op. cit.*; cf. C. W. Marshall, *Location! Location! Location! Choral absence and theatrical space in "Troades"*, [in:] *Seneca in Performance*, pp. 27-51.

[5] Cf. N. T. Pratt, *Dramatic Suspense in Seneca and his Greek Precursors*, Princeton 1939.

[6] Cf. Plin. *Epist.* 17, 17.

[7] The possibility that it was "only" read aloud does not, of course, exclude some gesticulation.

The only thing we can say with any certainty is that the plays are highly descriptive[8] and that narrative often takes precedence over drama (i.e. dialogue) and at times even substitutes itself for stage props.[9] Moreover, the plots themselves exhibit certain inconsistencies and these alone would make any stage performance somewhat problematic.[10]

What all this means is that there are parts of the text which are meant to be imagined by the audience, which is why in the nineteenth century scholars labelled Seneca's tragedies as *rhetorical tragedies*[11] or *Rezitationsdramen*.[12] Friedrich Leo pointed out that they were considerably different from the works of earlier Roman tragedians.[13] He also analysed their close relationship with declamatory rhetoric.[14]

Modern scholars have noted that Seneca's tragedies were strongly influenced by Latin epic, especially by Ovid's *Metamorphoses*.[15] Rainer Jakobi has devoted a whole book[16] to this difficult subject. For Seneca, Ovid is not only an inspiring source of myths and motifs, but also a model of style.[17]

It is not my purpose here to catalogue all the recent and older studies on Senecan tragedy. I will merely give a short account of the present state of research in order to review the most important opinions scholars have had on the subject — by which I understand the conclusions of those studies which have a direct bearing on the problems I intend to investigate.

---

[8] Cf. R. Stamm, *The Mirror-Technique in Senecan and Pre-Shakespearean Tragedy*, Bern 1975, p. 23.

[9] Although this was also a feature of Greek tragedy, in the case of Seneca's tragedies the descriptive element tends to dominate.

[10] Cf. E. Fantham, *Roman Literary Culture from Cicero to Apuleius*, London 1999, p. 151; cf. J. Fitch, *Playing Seneca?*, [in:] *Seneca in Performance*, p. 11.

[11] Cf. F. Leo, *De Senecae tragoediis observationes criticae*, Berlin 1879, passim. This line of investigation has recently been continued by Wolf Lüder Liebermann; see: *Senecas Tragödien. Forschungsüberblick und Methodik*, [in:] *Sénèque le tragique*, ed. by M. Billerbeck, E. Schmidt, Genève 2004, p. 39.

[12] Cf. O. Zwierlein, *Die Rezitationsdramen Senecas*, Meisenheim am Glan 1966.

[13] Cf. F. Leo, *op. cit.*

[14] Cf. *ibidem*, p. 158. This line of investigation has recently been continued by Wolf Lüder Liebermann; see: *Senecas Tragödien...*, p. 39. *Senecan tragedy is at once a product of its age, in which theatricality, on and off the stage, was endemic, and a product of the tragic tradition, from the theatricalization of tragedy under Pacuvius and Accius, and possibly the Augustan tragedians, to the reception of praetextae, in which the audience faced the task of interpreting competing realities. Contemporary rhetoric — declamatio and suasoria, especially as adopted by Ovid — served as a stylistic bridge between the plays of Accius and the plays of Seneca.* (M. Erasmo, *Roman Tragedy. Theatre to Theatricality*, Austin 2004, p. 123).

[15] Cf. R. Jakobi, *op. cit.*; cf. E. Pianezzola, *Ovidio. Modelli retorici e forma narrativa*, Bologna 1999, p. 29 ff.; cf. P. Mantovanelli, *Perchè Ovidio non si poteva fermare (Sen. Rhet. Contr. 9, 5, 17)*, "Classica Cracoviensia" 2000, 5, pp. 259-273; cf. A. Schiesaro, *The Passions in Play. "Thyestes" and the Dynamics of Senecan Drama*, Cambridge 2003.

[16] Cf. R. Jakobi, *op. cit.*

[17] Cf. *ibidem*.

Perhaps the most striking feature of Seneca's tragedies are the numerous narratives and descriptions, which are strongly reminiscent of epic poetry. Also present are certain other features which are very characteristic of the epic genre — and which have already been widely investigated by Renate Stamm,[18] Elaine Fantham[19] and other scholars.

One of the most important studies on Seneca's tragedies is that of Victoria Tietze Larson, who has shown beyond all doubt that — from a practical point of view — these works are to a large extent closer to epic poetry than to drama.[20] In what I see as a fundamental chapter of her book, Tietze Larson describes Senecan drama as a *hybrid mixture of "narrative" technique with dramatic genre*[21] and calls it *epic theatre*.[22]

Another expert on Seneca's poetry, R. J. Tarrant, has written in the introduction to his annotated edition of *Thyestes* that *Seneca's memory was filled with phrases and lines from Vergil, Horace and Ovid, and the influence exerted on him by these Roman "classics" was deep and persuasive*.[23] He also draws attention to the fact that *a more general debt to Augustan epic — to the "Aeneid" and the "Metamorphoses" — can be seen in the narrative passages in which Senecan drama so notably abounds*.[24]

It is my opinion that Tietze Larson and Tarrant[25] have largely mapped out the path leading to a better knowledge of the precise genre of Seneca's tragedies and, in the present study, it is my intention to proceed further down that path.

Yet another important study is the article by Otto Regenbogen, who draws attention to Seneca's peculiar fascination with pain and with both physical and mental sufffering.[26] The subject has also been commented on in passing by other scholars. Jan Smereka,[27] J. Park Poe,[28] Gary Meltzer,[29] Cedric Littlewood,[30] R. J. Tarrant,

---

[18] Cf. R. Stamm, *op. cit.*

[19] On the comparisons in Senecan tragedies see: Seneca, *Troades. A Literary Introduction with Text, Translation and Commentary*, ed. with an introd., transl. and comment. by E. Fantham, Princeton 1982, p. 43. Fantham has also drawn attention to the numerous inconsistencies in the plots of these plays, which themselves would constitute a serious obstacle to any stage performance.

[20] Cf. V. Tietze Larson, *The Role of Description in Senecan Tragedy*, Frankfurt am Main 1994, p. 43.

[21] Cf. *ibidem*, p. 53.

[22] Cf. *ibidem*.

[23] Cf. Seneca, *Thyestes*, ed. with a comm. by R. J. Tarrant, Atlanta 1985, p. 18.

[24] Cf. *ibidem*.

[25] Cf. idem, *Agamemnon*, ed. with a comm. by R. J. Tarrant, Cambridge 1976, p. 7.

[26] Cf. O. Regenbogen, *Schmerz und Tod in den Tragödien Senecas*, [in:] *Vorträge 1927--1928 zur Geschichte des Dramas*, ed. by F. Sachsl, Berlin 1930, p. 193.

[27] Cf. J. Smereka, *De Senecae tragoediis dinosis colore fucatis*, "Eos" 1929, 32, pp. 615--650.

[28] Cf. J. Park Poe, *An Analysis of Seneca's "Thyestes"*, "Transactions and Proceedings of the American Philological Association" 1969, 100, pp. 355-376.

[29] Cf. G. Meltzer, *Dark Wit and Black Humor in Seneca's "Thyestes"*, "Transactions of the American Philological Association" 1988, 118, pp. 309-330.

[30] Cf. C. Littlewood, *Self-Representation and Illusion in Senecan Tragedy*, Oxford 2004.

Norman Pratt,[31] Anthony J. Boyle,[32] Denis Henry and B. Walker,[33] Tietze Larson[34] and especially Alessandro Schiesaro[35] also frequently discuss aesthetic questions. A study which deserves particular mention in this context has been written by Renate Stamm,[36] who calls Seneca an *expressionist*.[37]

Mention must also be made of the doctoral thesis of Mary Braginton,[38] who very precisely categorizes and analyses all the supernatural elements that are found not only in Seneca's tragedies, but also in those of his Greek predecessors,[39] including those who were[40] and those who were not[41] his models.

A recent book by Schiesaro[42] contains a detailed analysis of the relation of *Thyestes* to Ovid's tale of Tereus in the *Metamorphoses*.[43] In this study Schiesaro discusses Seneca's attitude to Ovid as his main model.[44]

In my own investigation I have often drawn on the articles of the Paduan scholar Paolo Mantovanelli,[45] one of Italy's chief specialists on Senecan tragedy. Other studies which deserve mention are a detailed study of Ovid's descriptive technique by Jerzy Danielewicz and a study of Ovid's narrative technique by Emilio Pianezzola.[46]

---

[31] Cf. N. Pratt, *Seneca's Drama*, Chapel Hill 1983, p. 77 ff.
[32] Cf. A. J. Boyle, *Tragic Seneca. An Essay in the Theatrical Tradition*, London 1997, p. 20.
[33] Cf. D. Henry, B. Walker, *Phantasmagoria and Idyll. An Element of Seneca's "Phaedra"*, "Greece & Rome", Second Series, 1966, 13, 2, pp. 223-239.
[34] Cf. V. Tietze Larson, *op. cit.*, p. 89 ff.
[35] I am especially indebted to this work. Cf. A. Schiesaro, *op. cit.*, pp. 13, 17, 36-37, 59, 69, 131, 122, 141, 148, 165, 232, 235, 249, 256, 268.
[36] Cf. R. Stamm, *op. cit.*
[37] Cf. *ibidem*, pp. 23, 29, 34, 35.
[38] Cf. M. Braginton, *The Supernatural in Seneca's Tragedies*, Menasha 1933.
[39] Cf. *ibidem*, pp. 46-92.
[40] Cf. *ibidem*, pp. 46-70.
[41] Cf. *ibidem*, pp. 71-98.
[42] Cf. A. Schiesaro, *op. cit.*
[43] Cf. *ibidem*, pp. 70-138.
[44] Cf. *ibidem*, pp. 70, 71, 73, 77, 80, 83-84, 133, 188.
[45] Cf. P. Mantovanelli, *Le menadi immemori (Sen. Oed. 440 ss.). Sulle funzioni di un coro Senecano*, [in:] *Nove studi sui cori tragici di Seneca*, ed. by L. Castagna, Milano 1996; cf. idem, *Il prologo del "Tieste" di Seneca. Strutture spazio-temporali e intertestualità*, "Quaderni di Cultura e di Tradizione Classica" 1992, 10, pp. 201-216; cf. idem, *Lo strappo lungamente atteso. Il caso di Sen. "Oed." 961*, "Quaderni di Cultura e di Tradizione Classica" 1994, 12, pp. 89-97; cf. idem, *"Populus infernae Stygis". Il motivo dei dannati del mito in Seneca tragico*, "Quaderni di Cultura e di Tradizione Classica" 1993, 11, pp. 135-147; cf. idem, *El Hado, la casualidad, el reino (Notas a Sen. "Oed." 22 sigs., 980 sigs.; "Thy." 604 sigs., 32 sig.; "Oed." 882 sigs.)*, [in:] *Séneca. Dos mil años después. Actos del Congreso Internacional de su Nacimiento*, ed. by M. Rodríguez-Pantoja Márquez, Cordoba 1997, pp. 237-244.
[46] Cf. E. Pianezzola, *op. cit.*

On a purely theoretical plane, I have found Edmund Burke's famous treatise on the sublime and the beautiful[47] particularly stimulating, both as a philosophical guide and as a source of intellectual inspiration. I also owe a great deal to the books of Umberto Eco,[48] Henri Peyre,[49] Wayne Booth,[50] Harold Bloom,[51] Northrop Frye,[52] Roman Ingarden[53] and Mieczysław Wallis,[54] a Polish specialist in aesthetic categories whose works have recently been "rediscovered". In this context I should also mention some works which deal with the subject of *decorum* in Latin literature.[55]

As regards the cultural context, I must mention Gustave Le Bon,[56] Alison Futrell,[57] Roland Auguet,[58] Richard Beacham[59] and Donald Kyle[60] as authors of very complete studies of Roman games. General studies on the ancient theatre have also proved to be extremely helpful.[61]

Quot capita tot sententiae. There is a rich variety of studies on Seneca's tragedies. Some scholars have discovered a political code[62] in them, while others consider

---

[47] Cf. E. Burke, *A Philosophical Enquiry into the Origin of our Ideas of the Sublime and Beautiful*, ed. by D. Womersley, London 2004.

[48] Cf. U. Eco, *The Role of the Reader. Explorations in the Semiotics of Texts*, Bloomington 1984; cf. idem, *The Open Work*, transl. by A. Cancogni, introd. by D. Robey, Cambridge (Mass.) 1989; cf. idem, *Historia piękna*, transl. by A. Kuciak, Poznań 2005; cf. idem, *Historia brzydoty*, collective translation, Poznań 2007.

[49] Cf. H. Peyre, *Co to jest klasycyzm?*, transl. by M. Żurowski, Warszawa 1985.

[50] Cf. W. C. Booth, *The Rhetoric of Fiction*, Chicago 1961.

[51] Cf. H. Bloom, *The Anxiety of Influence. A History of Poetry*, Oxford 1973.

[52] Cf. N. Frye, *Anatomy of Criticism. Four Essays*, Princeton 1971.

[53] Cf. R. Ingarden, *Das literarische Kunstwerk*, Halle 1931; cf. idem, *O dziele literackim*, transl. by M. Turowicz, Warszawa 1960; cf. idem, *Szkice z filozofii literatury*, introd. by W. Stróżewski, Kraków 2000; cf. idem, *Wybór pism estetycznych*, ed. with an introd. by A. Tyszczyk, Kraków 2005; cf. idem, *The Literary Work of Art*, transl. by G. G. Grabowicz, Evanston 1979.

[54] Cf. M. Wallis, *Wybór pism estetycznych*, ed. with an introd. by T. Pękala, Kraków 2004.

[55] Cf. W. Tatarkiewicz, *Estetyka starożytna*, Wrocław 1962; cf. J. Styka, *Estetyka stosowności (decorum) w literaturze rzymskiej*, Kraków 1997.

[56] Cf. G. Le Bon, *The Crowd. A Study of the Popular Mind*, Dover 2002.

[57] Cf. A. Futrell, *Blood in the Arena. The Spectacle of Roman Power*, Texas 1997; cf. eadem, *The Roman Games*, Padstow 2006.

[58] Cf. R. Auguet, *Cruelty and Civilization. The Roman Games*, London 1994.

[59] Cf. R. C. Beacham, *Spectacle Entertainments of Early Imperial Rome*, Yale 1999.

[60] Cf. D. Kyle, *Spectacles of Death in Ancient Rome*, London — New York 1998.

[61] Cf. M. Bieber, *The History of the Greek and Roman Theater*, Princeton 1961.

[62] Cf. J. D. Bishop, *Seneca's Daggered Stylus. Political Code in the Tragedies*, Meisenheim am Glan 1985. This study has also been deemed controversial by Elżbieta Wesołowska (cf. *Seneka w oczach Władysława Strzeleckiego*, [in:] *Mistrz Władysław Strzelecki (1905--1967)*, ed. by L. Stankiewicz, Wrocław 2006, p. 75). The hypothesis that Seneca used his plays as a vehicle of political propaganda against Nero (cf. J. D. Bishop, *op. cit.*, p. 3) has been called *grotesquely naïve* by J. W. Calder III (cf. *Theatrokratia. Collected Papers on the Politics and Staging of Greco-Roman Tragedy*, ed. by R. Scott Smith, Zürich — New York 2005, pp. 317-318). See also: E. Wesołowska, *Seneka w oczach Władysława Strzeleckiego*, p. 78; E. Fantham, *Roman*

their characters to be exemplifications of the Stoic theory of virtues and vices.[63] There are also those who try to compare Senecan tragedy with Athenian tragedy.[64] Although I myself do not fully support all the methods used by these various scholars, there is no doubt that their studies contain many highly interesting analyses.

In the present study I wish to concentrate on Seneca's most significant literary techniques, such as his use of the achievements of epic poetry, the contrast technique, his peculiar aesthetic of disgust, his original use of the supernatural and on his *aemulatio* of literary predecessors. At the same time I will analyse and compare passages of Seneca's tragedies with other masterpieces written by authors living both before and after Seneca.

First and foremost, however, I would like to investigate the problem of Seneca's originality as an artist and his relationship with earlier Roman poetry. By means of detailed analyses of the most representative passages of his tragedies I hope not only to show how Seneca used the achievements of his predecessors to greater effect, but also to reconstruct his own literary and aesthetic *credo*.

This introduction would not be complete without a word of thanks to Prof. Elżbieta Wesołowska of the Adam Mickiewicz University in Poznań and to Prof. Mikołaj Szymański of the University of Warsaw, both of whom provided me with much valuable advice. I am also indebted to Dr. Andrzej Obrębski and Prof. Zdzisław Pietrzyk of the Jagiellonian University in Cracow, without whose encouragement and constant support this book would never have seen the light of day.

Literary Culture..., p. 150; J. Rostropowicz, *Władysława Strzeleckiego uwagi o aluzjach politycznych w niektórych tragediach Seneki*, [in:] *Mistrz Władysław Strzelecki...*, pp. 97-102.

[63] Cf. U. Knoche, *Senecas Atreus. Ein Beispiel* (1941), [in:] *Senecas Tragödien*, ed. by E. Lefèvre, Darmstadt 1972, pp. 477-489; cf. idem, *Eine Brücke vom Philosophen Seneca zum Tragiker Seneca* (1941), [in:] *Senecas Tragödien*, pp. 58-66; cf. E. Lefèvre, *"Quid ratio possit?". Senecas Phaedra als stoisches Drama* (1969), [in:] *Senecas Tragödien*, pp. 343-375; cf. idem, *Schicksal und Selbstverschuldung in Senecas Agamemnon* (1966), [in:] *Senecas Tragödien*, pp. 457-476; cf. C. M. King, *Seneca's "Hercules Oetaeus". A Stoic Interpretation of the Greek Myth*, "Greece & Rome", Second Series, 1971, 18, 2, pp. 215-222; cf. B. Marti, *Seneca's Tragedies. A New Interpretation*, "Transactions and Proceedings of the American Philological Association" 1945, 76, pp. 216-245; cf. W. Jamróz, *Herakles i Dejanira Seneki jako exempla*, "Meander" 1972, 27, pp. 64-79; cf. H. Hine, *Interpretatio Stoica of Senecan Tragedy*, [in:] *Sénèque le tragique*, pp. 173-209.

[64] This approach has been rejected out of hand by A. L. Motto and J. R. Clark in: *Senecan Tragedy*, Amsterdam 1988, p. 24.

CHAPTER I

An Imaginary Scene — Crossing the Frontier of Genre

But in the imagination, besides the pain or pleasure arising from the properties of the natural object, a pleasure is perceived from the resemblance, which the imitation has to the original; the imagination, I conceive, can have no pleasure but what results from one or the other of these causes.

Edmund Burke, *A Philosophical Enquiry into the Origin of our Ideas of the Sublime and Beautiful.*[65]

First of all, I owe my readers an explanation of the meaning of the title of this chapter. The term *imaginary scene* has been used by scholars to refer to the highly descriptive character of Senecan tragedy.[66] Those who use this term, however, are very careful not to label the plays as being completely non-theatrical.

Before I begin my attempt to reconstruct the aesthetics of Seneca's tragedies, I will have to look very closely at their structure and composition. I will also analyse Seneca's attitude to drama as an art, which will be rather difficult, as Seneca says practically nothing about his own poetry and very little about poetry in general.[67]

---

[65] E. Burke, *op. cit.*, p. 69.

[66] [Stamm about *Phae.* 702 ff.:] *Though the scene has a dramatic intensity in the impulse words, it is an imaginary scene which owes its effect to description.* (R. Stamm, *op. cit.*, p. 25). *The length and vividness of many of the descriptions suggest rather, that they often aim to replace the visible realities of the "stage"-situation with an imaginary scene which, even if the play were performed, could exist only in the mind's eye. As such then, their "modus operandi" is the narrative mode.* (V. Tietze Larson, *op. cit.*, p. 59).

[67] *Seneca, famously, almost never speaks of drama in his non-dramatic works, so his theoretical understanding of it can never be known.* (B. S. Hook, *Nothing within which passeth show. Character and "color" in Senecan Tragedy*, [in:] *Seneca in Performance*, p. 65). Unfortunately Seneca's tragedies are also virtually passed over in silence by Quintilian.

As far as drama is concerned, in letter 88 Seneca quotes the Stoic philosopher Posidonius, who divides the arts into four groups: *vulgares et sordidae, ludicrae, pueriles* and *liberales*.[68] According to this division, drama belongs to the second group, i.e. *artes ludicrae*:

> *Ludicrae sunt, quae ad voluptatem oculorum atque aurium tendunt. His adnumeres licet machinatores, qui pegmata per se surgentia excogitant et tabulata tacite in sublime crescentia et alias ex inopinato varietates aut dehiscentibus, quae cohaerebant, aut his, quae distabant, sua sponte coeuntibus aut his, quae eminebant, paulatim in se residentibus. His imperitorum feriuntur oculi omnia subita, quia causas non novere, mirantium.* (*Epist.* 88, 22)

As it obviously does not come under the other categories, it is quite clear that Seneca considered drama to be a kind of entertainment and — as a true Stoic — did not take it too seriously. Perhaps that is why there is no mention of his own tragedies in his other works. This being the case, it is quite possible that Seneca treated drama, and perhaps literature in general, in purely aesthetic terms. This would also explain why, though he disdained the amphitheatre, Seneca wrote plays which abounded in violence and the macabre:[69]

> *Nihil vero tam damnosum bonis moribus quam in aliquo spectaculo desidere. Tunc enim per voluptatem facilius vitia subrepunt. Quid me existimas dicere? Avarior redeo, ambitiosior, luxuriosior, immo vero crudelior et inhumanior, quia inter homines fui. Casu in meridianum spectaculum incidi lusus exspectans et sales et aliquid laxamenti, quo hominum oculi ab humano cruore acquiescant: contra est. Quidquid ante pugnatum est, misericordia fuit. Nunc omissis nugis mera homicidia sunt. Nihil habent quo tegantur, ad ictum totis corporibus expositi numquam frustra manum mittunt. Hoc plerique ordinariis paribus et postulaticiis praeferunt. Quidni praeferant? Non galea, non scuto repellitur ferrum. Quo munimenta? Quo artes? Omnia ista mortis morae sunt. Mane leonibus et ursis homines, meridie spectatoribus suis obiciuntur. Interfectores interfecturis iubent obici et victorem in aliam detinent caedem: exitus pugnantium mors est. Ferro et igne res geritur. Haec fiunt dum vacat harena. "Sed latrocinium fecit aliquis, occidit hominem." Quid ergo? quia occidit, ille meruit ut hoc pateretur: tu quid meruisti miser ut hoc spectes? "Occide, verbera, ure! Quare tam timide incurrit in ferrum? Quare parum audacter occidit? Quare parum libenter moritur? Plagis agatur in vulnera, mutuos ictus nudis et obviis pectoribus excipiant." Intermissum est spectaculum: "interim iugulentur homines, ne nihil agatur."* (*Epist.* 7, 2-5)

Paradoxically, moral convictions are not always mirrored by aesthetic taste. Mass slaughters and public executions in the arena repelled Seneca as a Stoic thinker, but as a Roman he found them quite fascinating.[70] Although Seneca strongly

---

[68] Cf. *Epist.* 88, 21.
[69] Cf. M. Kocur, *We władzy teatru*, Wrocław 2005, p. 78.
[70] Cf. M. Leigh, *Lucan. Spectacle and Engagement*, Oxford 1997, pp. 263, 281.

disapproved of the *ludi*, the favourite themes of his plays were murders, suicides and horribly mutilated corpses. Seneca's personal taste was strongly influenced by that of his fellow Romans.[71] Neither should we forget that, apart from sharing the tastes of his contemporaries, Seneca also had to take into account their sensibility. "Milder" plays would scarcely appeal to people who were accustomed to seeing horrible spectacles almost on a daily basis.

Notwithstanding their wildness and grossness,[72] Seneca's contemporaries had a particular fondness for declamatory rhetoric,[73] which meant that their imaginations were well developed and could easily be influenced by skilful oratory.[74] On the other hand, their peculiar taste for blood and cruelty required correspondingly bloody and cruel images (which in Seneca's case were verbal images).

Poets like Seneca or Lucan were not unaware of the great opportunity which they had been given.[75] They knew perfectly well that idyllic poems would make little or no impact on their contemporaries. They also knew that the aesthetic needs of an audience which had a taste for savagery and which at the same time had a powerful

---

[71] *Death as spectacle was a Roman pastime, and even though Seneca himself deplored it in an eloquent letter [...], he was to some extent infected by the taste.* (R. Mayer, *Seneca: "Phaedra"*, London 2002, p. 32). See also: M. Kocur, op. cit., p. 42. *Modern civilization surrounds the execution of criminals with a screen of secrecy; high prison walls, veils, an early morning or nocturnal hour, all have their part in concealing the act from the world of the living. This guilt-laden shame did not exist at Rome.* (R. Auguet, op. cit., p. 65).

[72] Cf. R. Mayer, op. cit., pp. 31-32.

[73] Cf. Petr. *Sat.* 1-2. *Several factors seem involved in the evolution of this style. One was Ovid. Another was the emphasis of rhetoric in the schools [...]. The "Controversiae" and "Suasoriae" of Seneca's father, which were probably written in the 30s CE, and must have had a profound impact on Seneca himself, document such declamations and indicate the kind of training the schools provided.* (A. J. Boyle, *Tragic Seneca...*, p. 21).

[74] *The plays are admirably adapted for declamation before an imperial highbrow audience of crude sensibility but considerable sophistication in the ingenuities of language.* (T. S. Eliot, *Seneca in Elizabethan Translation*, [in:] idem, *Selected Essays*, 2nd edition, London—Boston 1934, p. 68).

[75] *Within this iconosphere Senecan tragedy was created, structured by, even as it represents, the late Julio-Claudian world. That world and its cultural models are not always understood, especially its literary forms, which are often castigated as the forms of literary decadence or at least decline. The change which took place in Roman poetry between the early Augustan period and that of Nero, between the "classicism" of Virgil and Horace and the "post-classicism" of Seneca nad Lucan, is conventionally described as the movement from Golden to Silver Latin. The description misleads on many counts, not least because it misconstrues a change in literary and poetic sensibility, in the mental sets of reader and audience, and in the political environment of writing itself, as a change in literary value. What happened awaits adequate description, but it seems clear that the change began with Ovid (43 BCE to 17 CE), whose rejection of Augustan classicism (especially its concept of decorum or "appropriateness"), cultivation of generic disorder and experimentation (see, e. g. "Ars Amatoria" and "Metamorphoses"), love of paradox, absurdity, incongruity, hyperbole, wit, and focus on extreme emotional states, influenced everything that followed.* (A. J. Boyle, *Tragic Seneca...*, p. 20).

imagination were nothing if not special.⁷⁶ This may explain why their works contain so many highly visual scenes of violence and brutality. If we read Seneca's tragedies not as dramas, but rather as descriptive poems,⁷⁷ we will gain a better understanding of their cultural context and the peculiar taste of the early Roman empire.

Edmund Burke, the famous eighteenth-century theorist of aesthetics, has given an interesting philosophical explanation of this phenomenon. All dramatic poetry, he says, operates by imitation *(there is strictly imitation)*, while *descriptive poetry operates chiefly by substitution; by means of sounds, which by custom have the effect of realities.*⁷⁸

Let us remember that in the Rome of Claudius and Nero, epic poetry — and poetry in general — was as often as not read aloud in public. The listener had to imagine things which he could not see with his own eyes. His imagination was therefore rather different from ours. It was certainly more powerful — if only because there was no such thing as the cinema or television.⁷⁹

There was the theatre, of course, and there was also the amphitheatre, where real death was an aesthetic fact.⁸⁰ The peculiar pleasure of watching live spectacles of death derived from the fact that in an amphitheatre the spectators were safe and comfortable in their seats, while death and destruction raged in the arena below them.

One possible explanation for the obsession with death and decay which we observe in ancient Roman culture may be that people came to the amphitheatre to

---

⁷⁶ *To organize a text, its author has to rely upon a series of codes that assign given contents to the expressions he uses. To make his text communicative, the author has to assume that the ensemble of codes he relies upon is the same as that shared by his possible reader. The author has thus to foresee a model of the possible reader (hereafter Model Reader) supposedly able to deal interpretatively with the expressions in the same way as the author deals generatively with them.* (U. Eco, *The Role of the Reader...*, p. 7).

⁷⁷ *[...] for in general Seneca himself, a highly self-conscious stylist in prose and poetry, seems to have laid prime emphasis just there, and only secondarily attended to more conventional considerations of dramatic art. Indeed, one might argue that a fuller understanding of Seneca's peculiar qualities as a Latin poet is to be attained by ignoring the usual questions [...] and instead treating his works merely as poems — not portrayals of action, but verbal paintings of almost static situations well known to the reader, but depicted in ever fuller detail as the work progresses.* (D. Mastronarde, *Seneca's "Oedipus". The Drama in the Word*, "Transactions and Proceedings of the American Philological Association" 1970, 101, p. 291).

⁷⁸ Cf. E. Burke, *op. cit.*, p. 196.

⁷⁹ *It was certainly a central concern of his to move his audience, to rouse their feelings by representing passion [...]. He achieved this by means of an objective, epic kind of mirror-technique, which was not conceived for a stage performance. He "saw" his plays, not on a concrete stage, but in the purely imaginary theatre of his mind. He was therefore not bound by the limitations of the stage, but could go to extremes. Expressionism, in fact, was an important element in his mirror-technique, which stressed the supernatural quality of his characters and their passions.* (R. Stamm, *op. cit.*, p. 36).

⁸⁰ Cf. M. Kocur, *op. cit.*, p. 79.

watch death from a safe distance,[81] thus overcoming their fear of death and disfigurement.[82] It must be remembered that in ancient Rome it was relatively easy to be killed, mutilated or sentenced to death. This fear was so strong in people's minds that they needed to "get it out of their system" by watching the deaths of gladiators and animals in real life or — in the case of literature — by watching the deaths of imaginary characters (as perhaps Seneca did).

In Seneca's tragedies we find many naturalistic descriptions of violent death and terrible suffering. An excellent example of this aesthetic is the shocking account of the self blinding of Oedipus (915-979), where Seneca gives a highly visual and very precise description of the man's mutilated face.

That said, however, the parallel between Seneca's art and the amphitheatre only goes so far. Whereas the appeal of the amphitheatre was predominantly visual, Seneca's tragedies appealed to the audience's imaginations through their sense of hearing. Another difference was that the audience in an amphitheatre saw, heard and smelled real death, while Seneca's audience knew that what they were experiencing was merely a work of art and had to use their imaginations to "see", "hear" or perhaps even "smell" what the author wished to present to them.

The bloody descriptions in his plays are a substitute, as it were, for the real spectacles of death in the amphitheatre.[83] Perhaps in this way Seneca gave his audience an opportunity to come into contact with death in a more gentle manner. It may also have been his "sanitized" alternative to the all too real butchery of the arena, of which he highly disapproved as a Stoic philosopher.[84]

In Seneca's plays we also find numerous places that are strongly reminiscent of the realities of Nero's Rome.[85] In *Troades*, for example, the author describes a typical

---

[81] Cf. P. Plass, *The Game of Death in Ancient Rome. Arena Sport and Political Suicide*, London 1995, p. 26; cf. A. Futrell, *Blood in the Arena..*, p. 3; cf. M. Kocur, *op. cit.*, p. 79. *As ritualized versions of actions originally taken to ensure the survival and safety of the group, Roman blood sports legitimized, dramatically communicated, and reinforced the social and political order of the community.* (D. Kyle, *op. cit.*, p. 265).

[82] *The ideas of pain, sickness, and death, fill the mind with strong emotions of horror; but life and health, though they put us in capacity of being affected with pleasure, they make no such impression by the simple enjoyment. The passions therefore which are conversant about the preservation of the individual, turn chiefly on pain and danger, and they are the most powerful of all the passions.* (E. Burke, *op. cit.*, p. 86).

[83] *Given the prevalence of these horrific spectacles and their memorialization in Roman domestic interiors, Seneca's tragedies, with their similar emphasis on grotesque and macabre events, may have been intended to arouse the same reactions of horror, aversion, pleasure or titillation on the part of audiences.* (E. R. Varner, *Grotesque Vision. Seneca's Tragedies and Neronian Art*, [in:] *Seneca in Performance*, p. 127).

[84] *Seneca and his circle often commented on the slaughter in the arena, but from an elite, intellectual perspective.* (D. Kyle, *op. cit.*, p. 4).

[85] *Observation and vision, as well as the physical act of viewing are foregrounded and explored in fourth-style wall paintings. This interest in the process of viewing is analogous to Seneca's exploration of audience response to the bloody spectacles stages in arenas.* (E. R. Varner, *op. cit.*, p. 127).

public execution of the kind that were organized during Roman festivities. The following passage recounts the death of Astyanax, a young Trojan prince:

Haec nota quondam turris et muri decus,
nunc saeva cautes, undique adfusa ducum
plebisque turba cingitur; totum coit
ratibus relictis vulgus. His collis procul
aciem patenti liberam praebet loco,
his alta rupes, cuius in fastigio
erecta summos turba libravit pedes.
Hunc pinus, illum laurus, hunc fagus gerit
et tota populo silva suspenso tremit.
Extrema montis ille praerupti petit,
semusta at ille tecta vel saxum imminens
muri cadentis pressit, atque aliquis (nefas)
tumulo ferus spectator Hectoreo sedet.
(*Tro.* 1075-1087)

The image of the bloodthirsty mob could well be that of Roman spectators in an amphitheatre.[86] Seneca calls the Achaeans *spectator ferus*. Moreover, this description of a public murder is very similar to that in *Epist.* 7. Perhaps it is a subtle caricature of the behaviour of contemporary Roman *spectatores feri* during the *munera*.

Both depictions — in *Epist.* 7 and in *Troades* — bear marks of exaggeration and even caricature.[87] The spectators behave in a grotesque, beastly way. They climb up trees and cling to their branches like bunches of grapes — just in order to get a better view of the execution of Astyanax. It may well be that here Seneca alludes to the spectacles of death which were so popular in his day. He also plays a kind of game with his audience, offering their imaginations the lurid depiction of a public execution by substituting verbal ἐνάργεια for ὄψις.[88]

In *Troades*, Astyanax dies like a true hero. Instead of being pushed, he throws himself from the palace tower to meet his death:

sic ille dextra prensus hostili puer
ferox superbit. Moverat vulgum ac duces
ipsumque Ulixem. Non flet e turba omnium
qui fletur; ac, dum verba fatidici et preces

---

[86] *In his portrayal of the executions of Astyanax and Polyxena, Seneca presented to his Roman audience a situation which was similar to the events of the amphitheater.* (J. Shelton, *The spectacle of death in Seneca's "Troades"*, [in:] *Seneca in Performance*, p. 112).

[87] Cf. C. Littlewood, *op. cit.*, p. 254.

[88] *[...] And even if Seneca's dramas were not physically performed on a stage in all of their bloody detail, the visual evidence of fourth-style wall paintings suggests that their effects would have been easily pictured or imagined by Roman audiences.* (E. R. Varner, *op. cit.*, p. 132).

concipit Ulixes vatis et saevos ciet
ad sacra superos, sponte desiluit sua
in media Priami regna.
(*Tro.* 1097-1103)

This is what ancient Romans expected of gladiators.[89] And this is also what Stoic philosophers expected of their pupils: extreme courage and heroism. In one of his most important philosophical works Seneca himself draws a comparison between a Stoic hero and a courageous gladiator (*Const. sap.* 16, 2-3).

In the passage of *Epist.* 7 quoted above Seneca ridicules the brutal and ruthless mentality of his contemporaries. Here, however, he portrays their rather peculiar taste and their aesthetic needs. Like Astyanax, Hippolytus too is intrepid when faced with imminent death. He is an undaunted warrior who accepts his fate with defiance and heroic courage:

Hippolytus artis continet frenis equos
pavidosque notae vocis hortatu ciet.
Est alta ad Argos collibus ruptis via,
vicina tangens spatia suppositi maris;
hic se illa moles acuit atque iras parat.
Ut cepit animos seque praetemptans satis
prolusit irae, praepeti cursu evolat,
summam citato vix gradu tangens humum,
et torva currus ante trepidantis stetit.
Contra feroci gnatus insurgens minax
vultu nec ora mutat et magnum intonat:
"haud frangit animum vanus hic terror meum:
nam mihi paternus vincere est tauros labor."
(*Phae.* 1055-1067)

Of course, we cannot say with complete certainty what Seneca really intended when he composed these scenes.[90] All we know is that:
1. Astyanax and Hippolytus have no choice — they must die.
2. They show extreme courage and *contemptus mortis*.
3. They die in a spectacular way.

Seneca quotes Cicero to support his view of the ideal gladiator:

Gladiatores, ut ait Cicero [Cic. *Mil.* 92], *invisos habemus, si omni modo vitam impetrare cupiunt; favemus, si contemptum eius prae se ferunt.* (*Tranq. an.* 11, 4)

---

[89] Cf. A. Futrell, *The Roman Games*, p. 121.
[90] For the problems of interpretation see: Ch. Martindale, *Redeeming the Text. Latin poetry and the hermeneutics of reception*, Cambridge 1993, pp. 2-10.

Seneca compares a brave gladiator to a Stoic philosopher, whereas Cicero compares him to a good orator (Cic. *Orat.* 228).[91]

Seneca's characters therefore have all the qualities required of an ideal gladiator and their διάνοια meets the demands of contemporary Roman audiences perfectly. We know that Seneca did not approve of gladiatorial contests, but for some reason he was fascinated by them. As a Stoic moralist he condemned spectacles of death as being nothing short of public butchery, but as an artist he had a peculiar, wild taste which in great part was a product of his times. He was doubtless also aware of the fact that traditional poetry, with its moderate or mild aesthetic qualities,[92] would be of little interest to contemporary Romans, who had acquired a taste for brutality and violence.

The problem of death and cruelty in Senecan tragedy is, however, more complex than appears at first sight. To begin with, we must explain the role of the extremely detailed descriptions of dismembered bodies in the plays, for it is quite clear that — for some reason — Seneca set great store by them.

It is also quite clear that the composition of these plays strongly resembles that of epic poems.[93] It abounds in narratives and descriptions[94] which are intended to appeal to the sensual imagination of the listener. A good illustration of this is the Manto scene in *Oedipus*, which consists almost entirely of highly detailed descriptions of the entrails of a dead bull.[95]

These places in Senecan tragedy play the same role as similar places in an epic poem — they stimulate the imagination of the listener (or reader) to produce its own "performance" of the scene. For example, the reader of the Manto scene can, in his mind, see quite clearly what is happening to the dead bull.[96]

---

[91] Both use the image of a gladiator to describe their "heroes" — the ideal Stoic and the ideal orator — as Roman gladiators were generally held in great esteem and had gained the status of heroes (Tertul. *De spect.* 22). Cf. D. Kyle, *op. cit.*, p. 80.

[92] The terms "sharp aesthetic qualities" and "mild aesthetic qualities" were invented by Mieczysław Wallis (cf. *op. cit.*, pp. 197-213).

[93] Cf. V. Tietze Larson, *op. cit.*, p. 53.

[94] Cf. *ibidem.*

[95] *Thomas Rosenmeyer has made the essential point, namely that the power of the scene depends on the word, on the verbal description, whose effect is on the imagination.* (J. Fitch, *op. cit.*, p. 10, after T. Rosenmeyer, *Seneca's "Oedipus" and performance: the Manto scene*, [in:] *Theatre and Society in the Classical World*, ed. by R. Scodel, Ann Arbor 1993, pp. 242--243).

[96] *In the narrative mode, on the other hand, the story is not identifiable with any apprehensive reality and is observed at second hand through the mediation of the narrator, who acts as eyes and ears for the audience, or reader, who pictures it in the mind's eye.* (V. Tietze Larson, *op. cit.*, pp. 55-56). *The length and vividness of many of the descriptions suggest rather, that they often aim to* replace *the visible realities of the "stage"-situation with an imaginary scene which, even if the play were performed, could exist only in the mind's eye. And such then, their* modus operandi *is the narrative mode.* (*Ibidem*, p. 59).

Seneca's tragedies were not a simple continuation of Greek tragedy.[97] They came into existence as part of a greater, Roman literary context which in large measure is now lost to us. We know practically nothing about the *Thyestes* of Varius and the *Medea* of Ovid, who were Seneca's direct antecedents. Neither can we say anything about the plays of Pomponius Secundus, who was Seneca's rival. The only thing that we *can* be fairly certain of is that Ovid did not intend his *Medea* to be played out on a stage:

Carmina quod pleno saltari nostra theatro,
versibus et plaudi scribis, amice, meis:
nil equidem feci — tu scis hoc ipse — theatris,
Musa nec in plausus ambitiosa mea est.
(*Trist.* 5, 7, 25-28)

We also know that the tragedies of Pomponius Secundus were performed in theatres (*carmina scaenae dabat*, Tac. *Ann.* 11, 13), but that is not enough. We cannot read them to see to what extent they were written in the dramatic or the narrative mode.[98] All that we have are the wild, weird plays of Seneca, whose composition is highly eccentric and whose scenes abound in cruelty and the macabre, ghosts, infernal apparitions and violent passions.

There is no simple explanation for the presence and role of these peculiarities in Seneca's tragedies. They must be analysed in the light of the whole literary, historical, cultural and (at times) philosophical context.

In order to gain a better understanding of Seneca's tragedies, we must examine them step by step, beginning with an analysis of certain literary techniques which link them to epic poetry.[99] Having done this, we will be able to discuss further matters, such as the aesthetics of these tragedies, their relation to Ovid's *Metamorphoses* and several other problems of this kind.

---

[97] *Whatever the precise chronology of his tragic career, Seneca was clearly taking up a form that had already been thoroughly domesticated and in which Roman "classics" already existed and were recognized as such. Competition with the Greeks, in the sense that had been so urgent a century earlier, was therefore no longer an issue. Perhaps for this reason, Seneca's tragic corpus shows no sign of programmatically defining itself against a classical Greek set of standards or models.* (R. J. Tarrant, *Greek and Roman in Seneca's Tragedies*, "Harvard Studies in Classical Philology" 1995, 97 (*Greece in Rome: Influence, Integration, Resistance*), pp. 219-220); cf. idem, *Senecan Drama and its Antecedents*, "Harvard Studies in Classical Philology" 82, 1978, pp. 213-263.

[98] Whether a play is theatrical or suitable for performance is one thing. Whether it is more dramatic (i.e. relies more on the mutual interactions of the characters) or more epic (i.e. relies more on narratives and descriptions) is another.

[99] Fortunately, some scholars have already touched on this problem, especially Tietze Larson (cf. *op. cit.*, p. 53 ff.).

Senecan tragedy is a very interesting field of research because it is representative of the post-Augustan period of Roman poetry.[100] Before examining the process of Seneca's departure from Ovid — his *ancestral poet*[101] — and the birth of his own originality as an artist, I will confront the two poets' βίος θεωρητικός, i.e. their "theoretical existence", with their βίος πρακτικός, i.e. their "actual existence".

One thing we know for certain is that in Seneca's day poets had already begun to write recitation dramas, as is shown by the example of Ovid's *Medea*,[102] though we cannot unequivocally decide whether the plays were intended to be staged or not.[103] We can, however, examine their structure, texture, style and intertextual links — or, put more simply, we can examine the βίος πρακτικός of Seneca's tragedies.

I have already mentioned the strong affinity of Seneca's plays with the Augustan epic, and with Ovid's *Metamorphoses* in particular. My intention is to study all the aspects of the composition of these tragedies, beginning with genological issues and ending with questions of aesthetics.

Let us begin with those passages which — for purely physical reasons — obviously could not be staged, but whose role is to stimulate the listener's imagination. One of these is the moment when Medea has two visions: of Megaera (one of the Furiae) and of the ghost of her murdered brother Apsyrtus:

[...] *Quem trabe infesta petit*
Megaera? Cuius umbra dispersis venit
incerta membris? Frater est, poenas petit:
(*Med.* 962-964)

Even if Seneca had intended his tragedies to be performed in a theatre, it would have been rather difficult to stage this particular passage. It is therefore the perfect example of a "scene" which must be imagined by the reader. The figure of Apsyrtus

---

[100] *Senecan tragedy is a highly metadramatic form of theatre; that is, one highly self-conscious in its reflection on the nature and models of its existence. In this respect, Seneca's metapoetic concerns are clearly on a par with those that animate works such as Ovid's "Metamorphoses", or Lucan's "Bellum civile". After Vergil, poetry appears increasingly unable to resist the compulsion to mirror in its own body the process of composition and the narrative mechanisms that make it possible.* (A. Schiesaro, *op. cit.*, p. 13; cf. H. Bloom, *op. cit.*, p. 20 ff).

[101] Cf. H. Bloom, *op. cit.*, p. 20 ff.

[102] There are those scholars, however, who seem to overlook the sheer scarcity of ancient evidence regarding the recitation performances in Rome: [...] *The exception, of course, is Senecan tragedy, because of a widespread (although by no means universal) conviction that the plays of the Senecan corpus were written to be read, or at most recited, but not to be produced on the stage. This idea, which is unsupported by any ancient evidence, was first set forth by A. W. Schlegel in the first decade of the nineteenth century and has been maintained by some, but scarcely all, more recent authorities.* (D. Ferrin Sutton, *op. cit.*, p. 1).

[103] In my opinion the penultimate chapter of Mayer's short book (cf. *op. cit.*, pp. 97-103) provides the best conclusion to the discussion on the staging of Senecas's tragedies.

is hardly recognizable (*umbra incerta*)[104] because he has been brutally mutilated (*dispersis membris*). His image is therefore terrifying for the audience and even for Medea herself.[105]

Another such place is at the end of *Phaedra*, when slaves bring the mangled corpse of Theseus' son Hippolytus back to his palace:

[...] *Hoc quid est forma carens*
et turpe, multo vulnere abruptum undique?
(*Phae*. 1265-1266)

Seneca depicts this moment in a very naturalistic way. He even shows us Theseus desperately trying to put the limbs back together:[106]

Disiecta, genitor, membra laceri corporis
in ordinem dispone et errantes loco
restitue partes: [...]
(*Phae*. 1256-1258)

The description of the dead Astyanax in *Troades* is equally vivid and naturalistic:

soluta cervix silicis impulsu, caput
ruptum cerebro penitus expresso — iacet
deforme corpus. [...]
(*Tro*. 1115-1117)

In the context of Roman spectacles of death it would be quite ridiculous to stage this scene.[107] Senecan tragedies are more epic tragedies than works for the theatre.[108]

---

[104] Scholars wonder what *incerta* could mean: [...] *probably "faltering", taken closely with* dispersis membris, *but it might mean "dimly seen"*. (Seneca, *Medea*, ed. with an introd. and comm. by C. D. N. Costa, Oxford 1989, p. 156).

[105] Even if *Medea* had been intended for the stage, this passage was clearly not. The audience must therefore have had to content themselves with imagining the ghost: *In a state of delusion Senecan characters may perform the most cruel acts. Medea kills her sons while she has a vision of a horde of furies and of her brother's scattered limbs (*Medea *958 ff.)*. (R. Stamm, *op. cit.*, p. 32). Cf. M. Braginton, *op. cit.*, p. 40.

[106] Some scholars interpret Seneca's exaggeration in this passage as unfortunate: *S. lacked a sense of humour and he failed to perceive that an over-explicit description becomes funny or wearisome*. (Seneca, *Phaedra*, ed. with a comm. by R. Mayer, M. Coffey, Cambridge 1990, p. 195).

[107] *I do not believe that Seneca had anything other than recitation in mind, and that there are moreover features of his dramas which would be ludicrous if performed with the means available in his day*. (R. Mayer, *op. cit.*, p. 17).

[108] *The discontinuity of scenes within Senecan tragedy and other problems of hasty entrances and exits make them unsuitable for stage performance and show that Seneca did not intend them for this medium*. (E. Fantham, *Roman Literary Culture...*, p. 151).

In this context the role of the precise descriptions of death and disfigurement has another purpose: in all probability it is meant to stimulate the listener's imagination.[109] In the case of the ancient Romans this was not a difficult task. Their minds were all too full of what they had seen in the amphitheatres and so their imaginations were only too capable of producing gory images of dead or dying gladiators, together with their screams and the smell of blood.

Vivid descriptions like those of Apsyrtus, Hippolytus and Astyanax inevitably evoked scenes from amphitheatres, and so Seneca's audience probably had a double aesthetic experience: that of the description itself and that of the all too real image it evoked. Such is the power of descriptive poetry, which is capable not only of creating wholly unreal images in our minds, but also of making us relive events that we ourselves have experienced in the past.

Another fact which may serve as evidence that Seneca's main concern as a writer was with the narrative and descriptive parts of his text is the composition of his unfinished play *Phoenissae*, which is a good illustration of the change in the role of tragedy in Rome. This tragedy has no chorus, which would suggest that in Seneca's day the presence of the chorus in tragedies was purely conventional; indeed, it had already disappeared from comedies altogether.[110] The composition of *Phoenissae* would also seem to show that Seneca not only experimented with poetry,[111] but that he also attempted to create a new kind of drama whose purpose was akin to that of epic poetry.[112] He liked to substitute imaginary drama for real drama and narratives and descriptions for scenic action.[113]

---

[109] On communication by means of description see: M. de la Almudena Zapata Ferrer, *"Descriptiones" en las tragedias de Séneca*, "Cuadernos de Filología Clásica" 1988, 21, p. 380.

[110] *We have, moreover, a possible glimpse into his method of composition in the fragmentary "Phoenician Women" [...] and the most possible account for its condition is that the play was unfinished, and published after the writer's death in a collected edition of his dramas. If that account is correct, it shows that Seneca composed his dialogue portions first, and slotted in the choral odes only after completing the spoken parts of the drama. If there was no dramatic reason for an ode then he simply inserted one to mark the departure of one character and the arrival of another — though that in itself did not require a choral interlude, as we see from the hectic last act of his "Agamemnon". The fact is that the Chorus was still felt to be an essential feature in tragedy, as it no longer was in comedy [...]. So a Chorus there still had to be for the sake of the genre, even when it had ceased to perform a substantial role in the action. Seneca was not prepared to innovate and dispense with it altogether [...], but on the other hand he did not take much trouble to revitalise its role as an active character in drama.* (R. Mayer, op. cit., p. 35).

[111] Cf. W. Owen, *Commonplace and Dramatic Symbol in Seneca's Tragedies*, "Transactions and Proceedings of the American Philological Association" 1968, 99, p. 313.

[112] It must be remembered, however, that epic poetry has always been an inspiration for drama and *vice versa* — not only in antiquity, but also in the Renaissance. Cf. I. Bogumił, *Adaptacje sceniczne czy dramaty? Antyczny epos jako źródło łacińskich tragedii i tragikomedii przełomu XVI i XVII wieku*, Gdańsk 2007, pp. 12-51.

[113] *The description not only replaces the reality that a performance (theatrical, or recitational) could provide, with a world of the imagination, but this world is one which could not exist*

An Imaginary Scene — Crossing the Frontier of Genre

As we know, in an epic poem the story is conveyed to the listener via the narrator's account of what happened, whereas in a play most of the events are witnessed directly by the audience. In Senecan plays, however, a great many of the facts are *related* and *described* by the characters themselves, who therefore act as epic narrators — or, should we say, as a *collective narrator*. This would have been a great innovation in the field of Roman poetry: an epic drama,[114] Seneca's idea, however, was not without precedent: there had been a Greek poet, Lycophron, who had done something similar in his *Alexandra*, combining the epic and dramatic genres into one highly original form.[115]

Although Seneca chose to write in the dramatic genre, in which there was no distance between narrator and audience, he "borrowed" many techniques from epic poetry. The characters in his plays are both standard *dramatis personae* and epic narrators in their own right. We can therefore say that in his plays Seneca crossed two borderlines or frontiers:

1. The frontier of genre (in some sense)[116] as he used techniques which were typical of epic poetry in tragedies. In this way he combined the power of epic with the directness of drama.

2. The frontier of literature itself: by means of narration and description he stimulated the audience's imagination to recollect real events, especially the spectacles of death which were so popular in ancient Rome.[117]

---

as it is described: the sights to which the Fury draws the attention of Tantalus are so widely separated geographically that it would be impossible to see them all together. (V. Tietze Larson, *op. cit.*, p. 57).

[114] Cf. *ibidem*, p. 53 ff.; cf. E. Wesołowska, *Postaci w "Medei" i "Fedrze" Seneki*, p. 71.

[115] Cf. Lycophronus, *Alessandra*, ed. with an introd., transl. and comm. by V. Gigante Lanzara, Milano 2000, p. 23. Lycophron had actually done what Seneca did later. Alexandra acts both as the main character of the poem (and as such she is introduced at the beginning, v. 4-8; 28-30), and as a traditional epic narrator. Both Lycophron's and Seneca's works are extreme examples of *Kreuzung der Gattungen*. Cf. A. Barchiesi, *The Crossing*, [in:] *Texts, Ideas and the Classics. Scholarship, Theory, and Classicsl Literature*, ed. by S. J. Harrison, Oxford 2001, p. 156. Before Seneca there had also been Ovid with his *Remedia amoris*, an epic poem written in elegiac verse.

[116] *As for my own traditional idea of genre, I choose two basic tenets plus a refinement. The tenets are that poeple are inclined to imagine genre as something that straddles two oppositions, (i) content versus form, and (ii) literary texts versus society, discourse, institutions. I don't see much point in the whole debate if genres are not used to bridge those oppositions. The less obvious qualification is that "genre" can be used so as to reconstruct the productive conditions of a text or a tradition; to re-create, at the point of reception, some impression, or imagination, about the setting in which the text was originated and performed.* (A. Barchiesi, *op. cit.*, p. 150).

[117] This is a perfect example of Burke's theory of substitution (cf. E. Burke, *op. cit.*, p. 196). We can also explain this phenomenon using modern semiotics: *Form is perceived as a necessary, justified whole that cannot be broken. Unable to isolate referents, the addressee must then rely on his capacity to apprehend the complex signification which the entire expression imposes on him. The result is a multiform, plurivocal signified that leaves us at once satisfied and disappointed with this first phase of comprehension precisely because of its variety, its indefiniteness. Charged with a complex scheme of references mostly drawn from our memories of previous experiences,*

Seneca created a completely new form of tragedy in which the narrative and descriptive elements took precedence over dialogue, which is the essence of drama. His tragedies were primarily directed at the imagination of his ideal listener or reader — a Roman gentleman who was not only erudite in poetry, but who also had decadent tastes and a lively imagination.

---

we then refer back to the initial message, which will be inevitably enriched by the interaction between those memories and the signifieds yielded in the course of this second contact — signifieds that will already be different from those apprehended initially, given the new perspective and the new hierarchy of stimuli of this second approach. Signs which the addressee might have at first neglected may now appear particularly relevant, whereas those originally noticed may have dwindled in importance. This transaction between the memory of previous experiences, the system of meanings that has surfaced during the first contact (and will again reappear as a "harmonic background" in the second approach), and the new system of meanings that is emerging out of a second contact automatically enriches the meaning of the original message — which, far from being exhausted by this process, appears all the more fertile (in its own material constitution) and open to new readings as our understanding of it gets more and more complex. (U. Eco, *The Open Work*, pp. 36-37).

CHAPTER II

Seneca and the Epic Poets

Δεῖ μὲν οὖν ἐν ταῖς τραγῳδίαις ποιεῖν τὸ θαυμαστόν, μᾶλλον δ' ἐνδέχεται ἐν τῇ ἐποποιίᾳ τὸ ἄλογον, δι' ὃ συμβαίνει μάλιστα τὸ θαυμαστόν, διὰ τὸ μὴ ὁρᾶν εἰς τὸν πράττοντα·

Aristotle, *Poetica*[118]

In this chapter I have set myself two main goals: firstly, to examine more closely the connection between Senecan tragedy and Roman epic poetry, and — secondly — to analyse the most important epic strategies which Seneca uses in his tragedies.

The motto I have chosen for this chapter comes from the *Poetics* of Aristotle, a treatise which is often extremely helpful in any discussion of subtle, theoretical questions, especially those concerning the subject of genre. In the passage quoted above Aristotle explains the major difference between drama and epic poetry.

The epic narrator is one whose presence in the poem allows the poet to write without any limitations and fulfil all the whims of his fertile imagination, as he does not have to show the events on a stage. He can therefore invent monsters, ghosts and all kinds of peculiar things, whereas the playwright has to reckon with the technical possibilities of the stage. The playwright's imagination is therefore constrained by conditions prevailing in the theatre.

To give an illustration of this, let us examine one particular passage of the Manto scene in *Oedipus*, where Seneca uses the descriptive technique in order to show *the irrational* (τὰ ἄλογα):

infecit atras lividus fibras cruor
temptantque turpes mobilem trunci gradum,
et inane surgit corpus ac sacros petit
cornu ministros; viscera effugiunt manum.
(*Oed.* 377-380)

---

[118] Arist. *Poet.* 1460a.

This is a good example of how Seneca makes the most of literary techniques. Of course, *Oedipus* is a dramatic work, but Seneca wishes the dead bull to come back to life! This, however, is possible only in the narrative mode, so — in the audience's imagination — Seneca duly paints a picture of the bull rising from the dead.[119]

Another example is the apotheosis of Hercules in *Hercules Oetaeus*:[120]

virtus in astra tendit, in mortem timor.
Praesens ab astris, mater, Alcides, cano:
poenas cruentus iam tibi Eurysthaeus dabit;
curru superbum vecta transcendes caput
Me iam decet subire caelestem plagam*:*
inferna vici rursus Alcides loca.
Al. Mane parumper — **cessit** *ex oculis, abit,*
in astra fertur*. Fallor an vultus putat*
vidisse natum? Misera mens incredula est.
(*HerO*. 1971-1979)

As in the passage from the Manto scene quoted above, this scene clearly cannot be staged. In the Manto scene the whole event is concurrently related by Manto, while in the apotheosis scene the character who relates the story is Hercules' mother Alcmena.

These concurrent accounts are a substitute for traditional epic narration. Seneca's plays belong to the dramatic genre, so they do not have an omniscient narrator. This role has been entrusted to the *dramatis personae*, who give the audience a running account of everything they see.[121]

---

[119] Even Fitch (who considers Seneca's tragedies to have been meant for performance on stage) acknowledges this scene as being non-theatrical: *This scene, then, is not written with the practicalities of stage performance in mind. On the contrary, it is intended for* recitatio, *where its vivid and detailed descriptions would have a spectacular effect in the audience's imagination.* (*op. cit.*, p. 11).

[120] The authenticity of *Hercules Oetaeus* has been widely discussed (cf. G. Biagio Conte, *Latin Literature. A History*, Baltimore 1994, p. 416) and many scholars consider this play to be unauthentic (cf. E. Malaspina, *Pensiero Politico ed Esperianza Stoica*, [in:] *Sénèque le tragique*, p. 269). In this book I follow those scholars who treat it as an authentic work by Seneca: *It is widely believed that this play is not by Seneca, and there are some abnormalities of metre and diction that in my opinion have been considerably exaggerated. I have argued elsewhere that the work is Senecan and very late* [...]. (R. G. M. Nisbet, *The Dating of Seneca's Tragedies, with Special Reference to "Thyestes"*, [in:] *Oxford Readings in Classical Studies. Seneca*, ed. by J. G. Fitch, Oxford 2008, p. 370). Ettore Paratore was radical in his defense of the authenticity of *Hercules Oetaeus* (cf. *Der "Hercules Oetaeus" stammt von Seneca und ist früher als der "Furens"*, [in:] *Senecas Tragödien*, pp. 545-558). There is also an older study by Stanley Pease who makes a careful analysis of the major stylistic and verbal similarities between *Hercules Oetaeus* and the other plays (cf. *On the Authenticity of the Hercules Oetaeus*, "Transactions and Proceedings of the American Philological Association" 1918, 49, pp. 3-26).

[121] Greek tragedy also made use of epic strategies, but almost exclusively in the messenger speeches, where the messenger acted as an epic narrator: *His freedom of movement within the*

There is a very similar apotheosis scene in the *Metamorphoses* of Ovid, namely the apotheosis of Hersilia, which might well have been the model for the apotheosis in *Hercules Oetaeus*. Here, however, the event is related by the narrator, as the *Metamorphoses* belong to the epic genre:

Paret et in terram pictos delapsa per arcus.
Hersilien iussis conpellat vocibus Iris.
Illa verecundo vix tollens lumina vultu
"o dea (namque mihi nec, quae sis, dicere promptum est,
et liquet esse deam), duc, o duc" inquit "et offer
coniugis ora mihi! quae si modo posse videre
fata semel dederint, **caelum accepisse fatebor!***"*
Nec mora, Romuleos cum virgine Thaumantea
ingreditur colles: ibi sidus ab aethere lapsum
decidit in terras; a cuius lumine flagrans
Hersilie crinis **cum sidere cessit in auras***.*
Hanc manibus notis Romanae conditor urbis
excipit et priscum pariter cum corpore nomen
mutat Horamque vocat, quae nunc dea iuncta Quirino est.
(Ovid. *Met.* 14, 838-851)

The similarity between these two apotheosis scenes is striking. Let us look at the *loci communes* which they share:

Ovid:
caelum *accepisse fatebor — cum sidere* **cessit** *in auras*

Seneca:
me iam decet subire **caelestem** *plagam —* **cessit** *— in astra fertur*

In the *Metamorphoses* there is another apotheosis scene — that of Julius Caesar, which could also have been a model for Seneca:

Vix ea fatus erat, media cum sede senatus
constitit alma Venus nulli cernenda suique
Caesaris eripuit membris nec in aëra solvi
passa recentem **animam caelestibus intulit astris***,*
dumque tulit, lumen capere atque ignescere sensit
emisitque sinu: luna volat altius illa

---

scenes he describes, like his invulnerability amid the carnage, derives from a self-effacement familiar from epic, where the narrator has access to a wide variety of perceptual points of view and yet nowhere appears in the fictional scene. But, of course, unlike the epic narrator, the messenger claims to have seen the events himself. (J. Barrett, *Staged Narrative. Poetics and the Messenger in Greek Tragedy*, Berkeley 2002, p. 44). Seneca, however, extended the use of this technique to other *dramatis personae*.

flammiferumque trahens spatioso limite crinem
stella micat natique videns bene facta fatetur
esse suis maiora et vinci gaudet ab illo.
(Ovid. *Met.* 15, 843-851)

Ovid's Hersilia travels to heaven on a star and Caesar is carried by Venus, while Seneca's Hercules ascends to heaven on his own, aided only by the force of his virtue. This fact may also be interpreted as a demonstration of Seneca's self-confidence and independence as a poet.[122]

Seneca's innovation lies in the fact that while he composes a scene which is very similar to that in the *Metamorphoses*, he dispenses with the traditional narrator: the apotheosis of Hercules is related by one of the characters. This, in my opinion, is a very good example of ingenious literary *aemulatio*.

Seneca challenges the traditional theory of drama, as expressed by Aristotle, that a dramatic poet cannot permit himself the pleasure of fulfilling all the wishes of his imagination. He shows that, on the contrary, a dramatic poet can do whatever he likes simply by "borrowing" techniques from another genre.[123]

In the previous chapter I argued that Seneca crosses the frontier or borderline between two genres — drama and epic — and that his tragedies are actually more epic than dramatic. As we have seen, Seneca replaces the traditional epic narrator with narrators drawn on occasion from among the *dramatis personae*. It should not be forgotten, however, that in the *Odyssey*, the *Aeneid* or Ovid's *Metamorphoses*, the principal narrator occasionally allows "lesser narrators" to take the floor. Seen against this background, Seneca's innovation appears to be a perfectly natural development. Seneca "shares" the role of the traditional epic narrator among the characters of his plays, so that each of them tells a different part of the story.

There is another place in *Hercules Oetaeus* where we can observe how the characters in Seneca's plays assume the role of the epic narrator. This is the scene of the prolonged death of Hercules, where the hero describes his sufferings to the audience:

---

[122] *The intensification and the self-realization alike are accomplished only through language, and no poet since Adam and Satan speaks a language free of the one wrought by his precursors. [...]. What gives pleasure to the critic in a reader may give anxiety to the poet in him [...]. This anxiety [...] is the anxiety of influence [...].* (H. Bloom, *op. cit.*, p. 25).

[123] Epic poets such as Virgil also "borrowed" from drama. Cf. P. Hardie, *Virgil and Tragedy*, [in:] *The Cambridge Companion to Virgil*, ed. by Ch. Martindale, passim; cf. S. Stabryła, *Latin Tragedy in Virgil's Poetry*, Wrocław 1970, passim. Ovid also confessed to borrowing subjects from tragedy:
tempore deficiar, tragicos si persequar ignes,
vixque neus capiet nomina nuda liber.
(Ovid. *Trist.* 2, 407-408).
Cf. B. Gibson, *Ovid on Reading: Reading Ovid. Reception in Ovid, Tristia 2*, [in:] *Oxford Readings in Classical Studies. Ancient Literary Criticism*, ed. by A. Laird, Oxford 2006, p. 365.

He. Eheu quis intus scorpios, quis fervida
plaga revulsus cancer infixus meas
urit medullas? Sanguinis quondam capax
tumidi vigor pulmonis arentes fibras
distendit, ardet felle siccato iecur
totumque lentus sanguinem avexit vapor.
*Primam **cutem** consumpsit, hinc aditum nefas*
*in **membra** fecit, abstulit pestis latus,*
*exedit **artus** penitus et totas malum*
*hausit **medullas**: ossibus vacuis sedet;*
*nec **ossa** durant ipsa, sed compagibus*
discussa ruptis mole conlapsa fluunt.
Defecit ingens corpus et pesti satis
Herculea non sunt membra — pro, quantum est malum
quod esse vastum fateor, o dirum nefas!
(*HerO.* 1218-1232)

Now let us see Ovid's version of the scene:

Nec mora, letiferam conatur scindere vestem;
*qua trahitur, trahit illa **cutem**, foedumque relatu,*
*aut haeret **membris** frustra temptata revelli*
*aut laceros **artus** et grandia detegit **ossa**.*
Ipse cruor, gelido ceu quondam lammina candens
tincta lacu, stridit coquiturque ardente veneno.
Nec modus est, sorbent avidae praecordia flammae,
caeruleusque fluit toto de corpore sudor,
*ambustique sonant nervi, caecaque **medullis***
tabe liquefactis tollens ad sidera palmas
"cladibus" exclamat "Saturnia, pascere nostris!
(Ovid. *Met.* 9, 166-176)

Whereas in Ovid's version the sufferings of Hercules are related by the narrator, in Seneca's version they are related by Hercules himself.[124] As we can see, these two passages are very similar. Let us look closer at the peculiar sequence of words which Seneca has repeated after Ovid:

Ovid:
cutem — *membris* — **artus** — **ossa** — *medullis*

Seneca:
cutem — *membra* — **artus** — *medullas* — **ossa**

---

[124] *It was seen that the effect of the "narrative" use of description was an increased authorial presence in the tragedies which allowed Seneca to present his "view" (in a literal sense) of the action: description supplants the real circumstances of the "performance" with a world which exists only in the imagination and is seen by the audience through description rather than with their own eyes.* (V. Tietze Larson, *op. cit.*, p. 135).

In all probability this is Seneca's way of alluding directly to the appropriate passage of the *Metamorphoses*, thus leaving a verbal trace of sophisticated *aemulatio*.[125] Moreover, Seneca's choice of the passage is not accidental. He has chosen one of the more cruel and shocking descriptions of the decay of the human body — one of those very descriptions which make Ovid a great innovator in the realm of Roman poetry.[126]

There is one further interesting thing about these two descriptions: in Ovid's version the names of the parts of the hero's body are scattered all over the passage. By contrast, in Seneca's version they are ordered in a very peculiar way: each one of them is the second word in the line:

*Primam **cutem** consumpsit, hinc aditum nefas*
*in **membra** fecit, abstulit pestis latus,*
*exedit **artus** penitus et totas malum*
*hausit **medullas**: ossibus vacuis sedet;*
*nec **ossa** durant ipsa, sed compagibus*
discussa ruptis mole conlapsa fluunt
(*HerO*. 1224-1229)

Although this may be sheer coincidence, it does make Seneca's description seem more vivid than that of Ovid, emphasising the anatomical details as it does by placing them almost at the beginning of each line. What in all probability Seneca was aiming for was the effect of ἐνάργεια, thanks to which he could stimulate the reader's visual imagination more effectively.

Ovid was a master of detail[127] and Seneca could not compete with his precise descriptions, but he could at least beat his predecessor on his own battleground — that of sublimity and verbal expression. Like those of Ovid, Seneca's descriptions are precise, but they are ever so much more expressive.

This can be better understood in the context of Seneca's *Quaestiones naturales*, where he rebukes Ovid for describing the great flood in a shallow and childish way, using a style which is quite unsuited to such a sublime subject:[128]

---

[125] This is an excellent example of the *idem aliter referre* technique.

[126] On the subject of cruelty in Ovid see: K. Galinsky, *Ovid's "Metamorphoses". An Introduction to the Basic Aspects*, Oxford 1975, pp. 131-132.

[127] Cf. J. Danielewicz, *Technika opisów w "Metamorfozach" Owidiusza*, Poznań 1971, p. 30.

[128] Cf. E. Pianezzola, *op. cit.*, Bologna 1999, p. 204. Παρά γε τοῖς ῥήτορσι τὰ ἐγκώμια καὶ τὰ πομπικὰ καὶ ἐπιδεικτικὰ τὸν μὲν ὄγκον καὶ τὸ ὑψηλὸν ἐξ ἅπαντος περιέχει, πάθος δὲ χηρεύει κατὰ τὸ πλεῖστον, ὅθεν ἥκιστα τῶν ῥητόρων οἱ περιπαθεῖς ἐγκωμιαστικοὶ ἢ ἔμπαλιν οἱ ἐπαινετικοὶ περιπαθεῖς. (Pseud. Long. 8, 3-8, 4). Schiesaro also quotes letter 41: *This letter elaborates a defence of the sublime aesthetic appeal of terrifying image [...]. This identification of naturalness and aesthetic appeal paves the way for a full artistic exploitation of the psycogogic and aesthetic potential of negative characters, and, of course, of such a distinctly Senecan feature as the locus horridus.* (A. Schiesaro, *op. cit.*, p. 127).

> [...] *sicut illud pro magnitudine rei dixit: "omnia pontus erat, deerant quoque litora ponto"* [Ovid. *Met.* 1, 292], *ni tantum impetum ingenii et materiae ad pueriles ineptias reduxisset: "nat lupus inter oves, fulvos vehit unda leones."* [Ovid. *Met.* 1, 304] *Non est res satis sobria lascivire devorato orbe terrarum.* (*Quaest. nat.* 3, 27)

Although Seneca admired, imitated and emulated Ovid, he used poetic expression as a brilliant way of breaking free of his predecessor's all-pervasive influence.[129] Thus, in the monologue of the dying Hercules, he showed just how good he was at describing sublime things in a sublime manner.[130] Perhaps this little chink in Ovid's armour, which allowed Seneca to achieve artistic "emancipation", had contributed to the development of his original, lurid vocabulary and "hacking" style.

Let us now return to our subject and examine the prologue of Seneca's *Medea*. We can see that the prologue itself contains elements which are obviously epic: to begin with, there is an invocation:[131]

> *Di coniugales tuque genialis tori,*
> *Lucina, custos quaeque domituram freta*
> *Tiphyn novam frenare docuisti ratem,*
> *et tu, profundi saeve dominator maris,*
> *clarumque Titan dividens orbi diem,*
> *tacitisque praebens conscium sacris iubar*
> *Hecate triformis, quosque iuravit mihi*
> *deos Iason, quosque Medeae magis*
> *fas est precari: noctis aeternae chaos,*
> *aversa superis regna manesque impios*
> *dominumque regni tristis et dominam fide*
> *meliore raptam, voce non fausta precor.*
> (*Med.* 1-12)

Medea pleads with the marital gods to help her, but in fact she expresses her wish to take revenge on Jason by herself.[132] This is very reminiscent of the invocation in Ovid's *Metamorphoses*,[133] where the narrator appears to summon anonymous gods, but in actual fact merely uses this as a way of expressing his wish that his own plan be put into effect.

---

[129] Cf. H. Bloom, *op. cit.*, pp. 26-27.

[130] Nevertheless, Seneca, who was conscious of a long literary tradition and who was also strongly influenced by rhetoric, elaborated his own technique of creating the sublime. (J. Pypłacz, *The Terrible and the Sublime. Some Notes on Seneca's Poetics*, "Classica Cracoviensia" 2007, XI, p. 296).

[131] Cf. E. Wesołowska, *Prologi tragedii Seneki w świetle komunikacji literackiej*, Poznań 1998, p. 38.

[132] Cf. *ibidem*, p. 44.

[133] On the similarities between Ovid's tale of Procne and Seneca's *Thyestes* see: A. Schiesaro, *op. cit.*, pp. 70-138.

Let us compare these two invocations:

In nova fert animus mutatas dicere formas
corpora: di, coeptis (nam vos mutastis et illas)
adspirate meis *primaque ab origine mundi*
ad mea perpetuum deducite tempora carmen.
(Ovid. *Met.* 1, 1-4)

The function of the prologue of *Medea* seems to be similar:

Nunc, nunc adeste sceleris ultrices deae,
crinem solutis squalidae serpentibus,
atram cruentis manibus amplexae facem,
adeste*, thalamis horridae quondam* **meis**
quales stetistis: coniugi letum novae
letumque socero et regiae stirpi date.
(*Med.* 13-18)

Like the narrator in the *Metamorphoses*, Medea informs the audience of her intention. Ovid's poet wishes to write a *carmen perpetuum* on the subject of changing forms, whereas Medea wishes to kill Jason's mistress and her father. The poet requests that the gods help him in his plan of construction, whereas Medea summons the Furiae so that they can aid her in her plan of destruction. Ovid's poet is a creator, whereas Seneca's Medea is a destroyer.

This opposition is very similar to that of God (the ancestor poet) and Satan (the younger poet) in Bloom's interpretation of Milton's *Paradise Lost*. If we treat the Poet as the *porte-parole* of Ovid and Medea as the *porte-parole* of Seneca, the similarities between these two prologues are much clearer.[134]

There is another similarity between these two prologues: the motif of the Sun god, referred to by both poets as *Titan*:

Ovid:
nullus adhuc mundo praebebat lumina **Titan**
(Ovid. *Met.* 1, 10)

Seneca:
clarumque **Titan** *dividens orbi diem*
(*Med.* 5)[135]

---

[134] *Let us attempt the experiment (apparently frivolous) of reading "Paradise Lost" as an allegory of the dilemma of the modern poet, at his strongest. Satan is that modern poet, while God is his dead but still embarrassingly potent and present ancestor, or rather, ancestral poet.* (H. Bloom, *op. cit.*, p. 20).

[135] The same motif appears in Lucan's *Pharsalia*: *unde venit Titan et nox ubi sidera condit* (Luc. *Phars.* 1, 15).

This in my opinion is ample proof that the similarities between these two passages are not accidental and that the prologue of the *Metamorphoses* was in all probability the hypotext of the prologue of *Medea*.[136]

The practice of borrowing words or even whole phrases from other authors was not an invention of Seneca — this he learnt from none other than his master Ovid, who did the same with passages from speeches by his favourite orator Porcius Latro. Indeed, we are told this by Seneca's father in his *Controversiae*:

> [...] *nam Latronis admirator erat, cum diversum sequeretur dicendi genus. Habebat ille comptum et decens et amabile ingenium. Oratio eius iam tum nihil aliud poterat videri quam solutum carmen. Adeo autem studiose Latronem audiit, ut multas illius sententias in versus suos transtulerit. In armorum iudicio dixerat Latro: mittamus arma in hostis et petamus. Naso dixit:*
> *"Arma viri fortis medios mittantur in hostis;*
> *inde iubete peti."* [Ovid. *Met.* 13, 121-122]
> *Et alium ex illa suasoria sensum aeque a Latrone mutuatus est. Memini Latronem in praefatione quadam dicere, quod scolastici quasi carmen didicerant: non vides ut immota fax torpeat, ut exagitata reddat ignes? Mollit viros otium, ferrum situ carpitur et rubiginem ducit, desidia dedocet. Naso dixit:*
> *"Vidi ego iactatas mota face crescere flammas*
> *et rursus nullo concutiente mori."* [Ovid. *Am.* 1, 2, 11-12]
> (Sen. Rhet. *Contr.* 2, 2, 8)

What is interesting about Ovid's borrowing technique is that he incorporates whole sentences or lines in a form which he modifies in order to suit his own taste. Seneca, whose poetic talent developed in the shadow of Ovid's genius, does likewise. In antiquity this practice was called ἐξεργασία or *paraphrasis* and was part of the canon of popular rhetorical excercises which were designed to help young poets to master the skill of *inventio*:[137]

> *An vero ipsi non bis ac saepius de eadem re dicimus et quidem continuas nonnumquam sententias?* (Quint. *Inst.* 10, 5, 7)

Being the son of a teacher of rhetoric, Seneca made the most of the techniques he had learnt as a boy from his father, and perhaps this particular exercise had led him to undertake an *aemulatio* of Ovid and Virgil.

The prologue of *Medea* is a very good example of literary *aemulatio*. Firstly, Seneca imitates the formal structure of Ovid's invocation in the *Metamorphoses*. Secondly, he uses the same name for the sun god. Thirdly, he inverts the purpose of the whole invocation by making Medea pray for the exact opposite of what Ovid's Poet prays for.

---

[136] An additional argument in favour of this hypothesis is the fact that in the rest of the prologue Seneca uses the name *Sol* — not *Titan*.

[137] Cf. P. Mantovanelli, *Perchè Ovidio non si poteva fermare*, p. 261.

Let us look at another "epic" place in Senecan tragedy — the scene of the execution of Astyanax in *Troades*. This *play within a play*[138] is a sophisticated *aemulatio* of Virgil, the second hero of Seneca's literary pantheon. Here Seneca competes with the scene of the duel between Turnus and Aeneas in the *Aeneid*:

Virgil:
*Tum studio <u>effusae</u> matres et **vulgus inermum**
invalidique senes <u>turris</u> ac <u>tecta</u> domorum
<u>obsedere</u>, alii portis sublimibus astant.
(Verg. Aen. 12, 131-133)*

Seneca:
*Haec nota quondam <u>turris</u> et muri decus,
nunc saeva cautes, undique <u>adfusa</u> ducum
plebisque turba cingitur; totum coit
ratibus relictis vulgus. His collis procul
aciem patenti liberam praebet loco,
his alta rupes, cuius in fastigio
erecta summos turba libravit pedes.
Hunc pinus, illum laurus, hunc fagus gerit
et tota populo silva suspenso tremit.
Extrema montis ille praerupti petit,
semusta at ille <u>tecta</u> vel saxum imminens
muri cadentis pressit, atque aliquis (nefas)
tumulo **ferus spectator** Hectoreo <u>sedet</u>.
(Tro. 1075-1087)*

Here too we can see a peculiar sequence of words which Seneca has repeated after Virgil:

Virgil:
<u>*effusae*</u> — ***vulgus inermum*** — <u>*turris*</u> — <u>*tecta*</u> — <u>*obsedere*</u>

Seneca:
<u>*turris*</u> — <u>*adfusa*</u> — <u>*tecta*</u> — ***ferus spectator*** — <u>*sedet*</u>.

In all probability Seneca here is emulating Virgil. Apart from repeating a sequence of words, he inverts one motif, as he does in the invocation of *Medea*. Whereas in *Medea* he inverts the motif of prayer, here he inverts the motif of the audience. In Virgil's version the audience consists of women and defenceless civilians, while in Seneca's version we have fierce spectators.

In my opinion this exact reversal from *vulgus inermum* to *spectator ferus* would seem to indicate that in this passage Seneca consciously challenges his predeces-

---

[138] Cf. C. Littlewood, *op. cit.*, p. 252.

sor. The inversion of motifs in both passages can hardly have been a coincidence. Moreover, Virgil's description of the spectators is given in a mere three lines, while that of Seneca is much longer. Indeed, Seneca describes the audience in quite an exaggerated manner. The spectators are literally everywhere, standing on the hills, climbing the collapsing walls of Troy, clinging to branches of trees and some even sitting on Hector's tomb. This is perhaps a caricature of Seneca's contemporaries, whose appetite for cruel spectacles he disdained,[139] though *he was to some extent infected by the taste.*[140]

What is more, Seneca's description is reminiscent of an epic catalogue. It contains a list of spectators (*his ... his ... hunc ... hunc ...*), together with information about their precise location. It is a particularly grotesque catalogue which borders on parody. This, however, was no innovation of Seneca's, for such peculiar catalogues had already appeared in the *Iliad*.[141] Its presence here is nevertheless noteworthy in that it is yet another borrowing from epic poetry.

Seneca here plays a very sophisticated game with his listeners or readers. He superimposes an original scene over a well-known passage of the *Aeneid* (which he is emulating).[142] Whereas in Virgil's epic poem this motif is quite insignificant, in Seneca's drama it is a key motif. Moreover, the description of the spectators in *Troades* even contains a little catalogue!

Seneca chose the epic mode to present the death of Astyanax because he knew that a messenger's speech would convey the πάθος of this scene better than a direct

---

[139] Cf. *Epist.* 7, 4-5. *The* ferus spectator, *a paradigmatic figure, blends together elements from within and without the dramatic illusion. The Roman colouring of* plebisque turba cingitur *(1077) encourages the natural identification of the real (or virtual) audience of the play with the audience inscribed [...].* (C. Littlewood, op. cit., p. 246).

[140] Cf. R. Mayer, op. cit., p. 32.

[141] E.g. the catalogue of animals in Hom. *Il.* 16, 149; the catalogue of nymphs in Hom. *Il.* 18, 39-49; and the catalogue of Achilles' horses in Hom. *Il.* 19, 400.

[142] As Boyle has noted, Seneca's *Troades*, as well as his other tragedies, are literary palimpsests: *Beneath each Senecan tragedy are a host of subtexts — Greek and Roman, Attic, Hellenistic, republican, Augustan and early imperial — clarifying and informing their discourse. In "Troades", for example, almost as a pointer to the play's concern with the recycling of history, Seneca rewrites and recycles many texts: most obviously, Homer's "Ilias", the cyclic epics, Sophocles' "Polyxena", Euripides' "Andromache", "Hecuba", "Troades" and "Iphigenia at Aulis", Naevius' "Andromacha", Ennius' "Iphigenia", "Hecuba" and "Andromacha", Accius' "Astyanax" and "Hecuba", Lucretius' "De Rerum Natura" 3, Catullus' "Peleus and Thetis", Horace's "Odes" 3.30, Virgil's "Aeneid", Ovid's "Metamorphoses", and (possibly) his own "Agamemnon". And "Troades" rewrites and recycles these texts self-consciously. Overt textual allusion and metaliterary language make of "Troades" a self-reflective, multi-referential text, which engages in a constant and persuasive counterpoint with the dramatic and poetic tradition.* (Tragic Seneca..., p. 89). Cf. W. M. Calder III, *Originality in Seneca's "Troades"*, "Classical Philology" 1970, 65, 2, pp. 75-82). Some scholars even look for the influence of Stoic writing on Seneca's tragedies (cf. B. Marti, *The Prototypes of Seneca's Tragedies*, "Classical Philology" 1947, 42, 1, pp. 1-16). For my part, however, I have centred on Seneca's allusive and emulative relationship to the works of the Augustan epic poets.

presentation.¹⁴³ The difference between narratives in a drama and the narration in an epic poem is that the distance which separates the reader from the events is smaller (*a few years ago...* or *a while ago...*) in the former and much larger (*a long time ago...*) in the latter. This is perhaps why Seneca preferred the dramatic form to the epic. His tragedies are more narrated than presented directly, but they are more persuasive as tragedies than they would have been as epic poems, since the narrators are not "transparent" (as they are in an epic poem) but are part of the play's "represented world".¹⁴⁴

In the tragedies of Seneca, therefore, the *dramatis personae* play a dual role: they constitute the action of the play and at the same time they are non-anonymous narrators who communicate all the past, present and sometimes future events to the audience. These narrators not only relate events, but — being individual characters in their own right — they tell their stories from their own personal points of view. A good example of this strategy is the monologue of Medea, in which she blames Creo for her misfortune (*Culpa est Creontis tota, Med.* 143).

In the works of the epic poets the action of the poem is dominated by the omniscient narrator who does sometimes allow the characters to tell their own stories, but only under his strict supervision. In a classical drama things happen *hic et nunc* and narratives are needed only to present those events which cannot be presented directly on the stage. Seneca's plays are different. Here all the events are narrated by the participants or by eye-witnesses and this is why these tragedies — though more epic than dramatic, narrated more than acted out — are as lively and direct as any classical drama.

The passage of *Hercules Oetaeus* analysed above shows us that no omniscient narrator could tell the audience about Hercules' pain better than Hercules himself. Seneca's version of this scene is more expressive than that of Ovid, not only because of his great rhetorical skill, but also because we learn everything *hic et nunc* from the dying Hercules, while in Ovid's version we learn everything from the narrator.

The same happens in *Medea*. In Ovid's version of the myth the narrator tells us Medea's story, while in Seneca's version we hear it from Medea herself and from her particular point of view. She tells us her story twice: in the *parodos* (*Med.* 116--149) and later, during her conversation with Creo. Each time she gives us new facts and does not repeat anything. Moreover, there is no chronological order in her narration¹⁴⁵ — the events are arranged in the order of their significance.

The monologue in which Medea presents the first chapter of her story gives us an outline of the *Vorgeschichte*:

---

¹⁴³ [...] *since the vehicle of narration allows descriptive interpretation of the motives of the child and the girl which their direct speech or dumb show on stage could not convey so articulately.* (Seneca, *Troades*..., p. 36).

¹⁴⁴ Cf. R. Ingarden, *The Literary Work of Art*, p. 230; cf. W. C. Booth, *op. cit.*, p. 211 ff.

¹⁴⁵ On the problem of time in Seneca's tragedies see: E. A. Schmidt, *Zeit und Raum in Senecas Tragödien*, [in:] *Sénèque le tragique*, pp. 321-356.

> *Si quod Pelasgae, si quod urbes barbarae*
> *novere facinus quod tuae ignorent manus,*
> *nunc est parandum. scelera te hortentur tua*
> *et cuncta redeant: inclitum regni decus*
> *raptum et nefandae virginis parvus comes*
> *divisus ense, funus ingestum patri*
> *sparsumque ponto corpus et Peliae senis*
> *decocta aeno membra:* [...]
> (*Med.* 127-134)

Medea's language is highly emotional (e.g. *scelera, nefanda*) and her narration is very expressive, especially when she speaks of the crimes she has committed, so that the listener can almost see the corpse of Apsyrtus being cut up into pieces and that of Pelias being cooked in a cauldron (*divisus ense, sparsumque ponto corpus, decocta aeno membra*).

The ancient Romans had a particular fondness for watching acts of cruelty.[146] It was therefore quite natural for them to take pleasure in imagining such acts. This is perhaps why Seneca was so ready to show scenes of murder and suffering.[147] In the passage quoted above he uses language to make the audience imagine the murder of Pelias.

During her conversation with Creo Medea reveals more details of her biography, such as the name of her ancestor (*Sole deduxi genus*) and the geographical location of her father's kingdom (*hoc omne noster genitor imperio regit*):

> *avoque clarum Sole deduxi genus.*
> *Quodcumque placidis flexibus Phasis rigat*
> *Pontusque quidquid Scythicus a tergo videt,*
> *palustribus qua maria dulcescunt aquis,*
> *armata peltis quidquid exterret cohors*
> *inclusa ripis vidua Thermodontiis,*
> *hoc omne noster genitor imperio regit.*
> (*Med.* 210-216)

This information should have been given at the very beginning, but Seneca chose to start his play with a shocking and expressionistic[148] image of murder in

---

[146] One interesting hypothesis is that this fascination with the amphitheatre had a deeper religious dimension connected with human sacrifice (cf. A. Futrell, *Blood in the Arena...*, p. 169 ff.).

[147] Scholars have already noted that in Seneca's plays there is a strong connection between *nefas* and aesthetic pleasure. This is what Schiesaro writes about *Thyestes*: *And there is an interesting hypothesis that their fascination with the amphitheater had a deeper religious meaning and could be understood in the context of human sacrifice.* (*op. cit.*, p. 37).

[148] *In the first place, the expressionistic artists assume that the surface aspects of things in no way reveal their essential nature. The surfaces of objects are static and the essential nature is dynamic.* [...] *Were we to ask the expressionist how he knows the essential nature of things, he would reply that this knowledge is attained by an emotional reaction to objects. Emotion gets be-*

order to rivet the attention of his listeners. Moreover, Medea's chaotic narration mirrors her savage and violent character.

There are also similarities between Seneca's *Medea* and Ovid's version of the myth in the *Metamorphoses*. Here too we find a peculiar *sphragis* by means of which Seneca alludes to the passage of Ovid that he is currently emulating:

Ovid:
[...] *per sacra **triformis***
ille deae, lucoque foret quod numen in illo,
perque patrem soceri cernentem cuncta futuri
eventusque suos et tanta pericula iurat;
(Ovid. *Met.* 7, 94-97)

Seneca:
tacitisque praebens conscium sacris iubar
***Hecate triformis**, quosque iuravit mihi*
deos Iason, quosque Medeae magis
fas est precari: [...]
(*Med.* 6-9)

Like Ovid's Medea, Seneca's Medea invokes the goddess *Hecate triformis* and all the gods by whom Jason swore fidelity to her when they were married. This is the second place in *Medea* where Seneca directly refers to the object of his emulation. This time he refers not to the prologue of the whole poem, but to the myth of Medea itself.

A few lines later there is another *sphragis* — which this time is quite obvious:

Ovid:
[...] ***Vivat** an ille*
occidat, in dis est; vivat tamen! Idque precari
vel sine amore licet; quid enim commisit Iason?
(Ovid. *Met.* 7, 23-25)

Seneca:
[...] *Si potest, **vivat** meus,*
ut fuit, Iason; si minus, vivat tamen
memorque nostri muneri parcat meo.
(*Med.* 140-142)

Let us look at the sequence of words repeated by Seneca:

---

yond the static surface aspect to the dynamic essence. (M. S. Harris, *Two Postulates of Expressionism*, "The Journal of Philosophy" 1929, 26, 8, p. 211).

Ovid:
vivat — <u>vivat tamen</u> — *Iason*

Seneca:
vivat — *Iason* — <u>vivat tamen</u>

This repetition can be no coincidence, especially in view of the fact that Seneca has repeated the same words in the same grammatical forms, almost in the same order and ... from the same story![149] This in my opinion shows that Seneca is here playing a sophisticated, intertextual game with Ovid. The participants of this game are, however, not only the dead Ovid and his younger rival Seneca, but also the audience — Roman noblemen who knew the *Aeneid* and the *Metamorphoses* off almost by heart. This kind of audience would immediately recognize the hidden quotations and thus understand Seneca's literary allusions as well as his *aemulatio*.[150]

It is a great pity that Ovid's tragedy *Medea* is lost, because without it we cannot judge whether Seneca — in his version of the story of Medea — is mainly imitating the epic version from the *Metamorphoses* or that lost tragedy, or perhaps both of them. All we can do is trace the *sphragides* Seneca has left and in this way attempt to reconstruct his path of ingenious emulation.

In *Medea* there are some more hidden quotations which are worth noting. The first of them is a single line with the motif of vengeance and escape:

Ovid:
<u>ultaque</u> *se male mater Iasonis* **effugit** *arma*
(Ovid. *Met.* 7, 397)

Seneca:
[...] *Me.* **Fugiam**, *at* <u>ulciscar</u> *prius*
(*Med.* 172).

The other quotation is even more interesting, because here Seneca directly emulates Ovid's account of Medea's nocturnal journey in pursuit of poisonous herbs:

Ovid:
Tres aberant **noctes**, *ut cornua tota coirent*

---

[149] The striking similarity between these passages has already been noted by Jakobi, though he does not focus on the subtle verbal *sphragis* (cf. *op. cit.*, p. 51). C. D. N. Costa has also noted that the possessive pronoun "mine" (ἐμόν) appeared in the *Medea* of Euripides (πατέρα τε καὶ κόρην πόσιν τ' ἐμόν, Eur. *Med.* 375, cf. Seneca, *Medea*, p. 84). Here Seneca is obviously imitating Ovid and not Euripides.

[150] *In any event, the relationship between* aemulatio *and allusion is asymmetrical. Emulation (at least in its most direct form) cannot exist without allusion, whereas allusion has no necessary connection with emulation.* (G. Biagio Conte, *The Rhetoric of Imitation. Genre and Poetic Memory in Virgil and Other Latin Poets*, transl. by Ch. Segal, New York 1986, p. 36).

*efficerentque orbem. Postquam plenissima fulsit
et solida terras spectavit imagine luna,
egreditur tectis vestes <u>induta</u> recinctas,
<u>nuda pedem</u>, nudos umeris **infusa capillos**,
fertque vagos mediae per muta silentia noctis
incomitata gradus.* [...]
*ter se convertit, ter sumptis fl umine crinem
inroravit <u>aquis</u> ternisque ululatibus ora
solvit* [...]
(Ovid. *Met.* 7, 179-185, 189-191)

Seneca:
*Nunc meis vocata sacris, **noctium** sidus, veni
pessimos <u>induta</u> vultus, fronte non una minax.
Tibi more gentis vinculo **solvens comam**
secreta <u>nudo</u> nemora lustravi <u>pede</u>
et evocavi nubibus siccis <u>aquas</u>*
(*Med.* 750-754)

These two passages are clearly very similar. As in the passages previously quoted, Seneca has left a *sphragis* in the form of a sequence of repeated words:

Ovid:
noctes — <u>induta</u> — <u>nuda pedem</u> — **infusa capillos** — <u>aquis</u>

Seneca:
noctium — <u>induta</u> — **solvens comam** — <u>nudo ... pede</u> — <u>aquas</u>

This time Seneca is very precise. He even repeats the whole phrase *nuda pedem*, changing only the *accusativus limitationis* into the *ablativus modi* and using different words to describe Medea's hair hanging loose (*infusa capillos* instead of *solvens comam*).

The passage quoted above is not part of the account of the gathering of herbs (which is related earlier by Medea's servant — *Med.* 670-739), but of Medea's monologue. The narration is therefore divided between two narrators: the *nutrix* and Medea herself, while in Ovid the whole scene is related by the anonymous narrator.

In this chapter I have concentrated mainly on *Medea* because it is an excellent example of an intertextual masterpiece, but Ovid is not the only poet whom Seneca emulates in this play. Let us look at the following two passages, the first of which belongs to the fourth book of Virgil's *Aeneid*.[151] It is part of the scene in which Dido, who has been abandoned by Aeneas, asks her sister Anna for advice:

---

[151] On Seneca's use of the fourth book of Virgil's *Aeneid* see: E. Fantham, *Virgil's Dido and Seneca's Tragic Heroines*, "Greece & Rome", Second Series, 1975, 22, 1, pp. 1-10.

Virgil:
en, quid ago? Rursusne procos inrisa priores
*experiar Nomadumque **petam** conubia supplex,*
<u>quos</u> ego sim totiens iam dedignata maritos?
Iliacas igitur classes atque ultima Teucrum
*iussa **sequar**? Quiane auxilio iuvat ante levatos*
et bene apud memores veteris stat gratia facti?
<u>Quis</u> me autem, fac velle, sinet ratibusve superbis
invisam accipiet? Nescis heu, perdita, necdum
Laomedonteae sentis periuria gentis?
Quid tum? Sola fuga nautas comitabor ovantis,
an <u>Tyriis</u> omnique manu stipata meorum
inferar et quos Sidonia vix urbe revelli,
rursus agam pelago et ventis dare vela iubebo?
(Verg. *Aen*. 4, 534-546)

Seneca:
*Ad quos remittis? Phasin et <u>Colchos</u> **petam***
patriumque regnum quaeque fraternus cruor
perfudit arva? <u>Quas</u> peti terras iubes?
<u>Quae</u> maria monstras? Pontici fauces freti
per quas revexi nobilem regum manum
*adulterum **secuta** per Symplegadas?*
<u>Patruamne Iolcon</u>, Thessala an Tempe petam?
Quascumque aperui tibi vias, clausi mihi
quo me remittis? Exuli exilium imperas
nec das. Eatur. [...]
(*Med*. 451-460)

Let us look at the *sphragis:*

Virgil:
petam — <u>quos</u> — **sequar** — <u>quis</u> — <u>Tyriis</u>

Seneca:
<u>Colchos</u> — **petam** — <u>quas</u> — <u>quae</u> — **secuta** — <u>patruamne Iolcon</u>

This time Seneca's game has become even more sophisticated, as here he is emulating not an epic, but a dramatic structure, i.e. a normal monologue, which is part of an epic poem!

Moreover, Seneca's Medea finds herself in the same situation as Virgil's Dido: she is a barbarian who has been betrayed and abandoned by her lover (who is a non-barbarian) and now considers the possibility of returning to her homeland, where she is not welcome.

The two characters are therefore in the same situation and... say almost the same things. The passages above have the same formal structure: they are both dramatic monologues and consist of short, desperate, rhetorical questions.

Seneca repeats this motif in *Hercules Oetaeus* in the scene where Alcmena laments the death of her son. I will quote only the first two lines of her monologue:[152]

Petam Cleonas? Arcadum an populos petam
meritisque terram nobilem quaeram tuis?
(*HerO.* 1811-1812)

In general terms, therefore, Seneca's method of emulation consists of three stages:
1. From an "ancestor poem" he chooses:
a) an entire myth (e.g. the myth of Medea — from the *Metamorphoses*)[153]
b) a motif (e.g. the motif of a betrayed barbarian woman — from the *Aeneid*).
2. He then chooses passages which he is going to emulate (e.g. the gathering of herbs from the *Metamorphoses* or the monologue of Dido from the *Aeneid*).
3. He leaves a *sphragis* in the form of a verbal sequence as a clue for his readers.

Let us now leave *Medea* and take a look at *Agamemnon*. Here we can find a very interesting passage — the ῥῆσις ἀγγελική of Euribates (*Ag.* 421-588). It is natural that messenger speeches are the most epic parts of a drama, but this one is particularly interesting because of the element of *aemulatio* it contains. This is the description of a sea tempest which is very similar to the one in Virgil's *Aeneid* and is a good example of Seneca's stylistic emulation:

Virgil:
Incubuere *mari totumque a sedibus imis*
una **Eurusque Notusque** *ruunt creberque procellis*
Africus et vastos **volvunt** *ad litora* **fluctus**.
[...]
Talia iactanti stridens **Aquilone** *procella*
velum adversa ferit, fluctusque ad sidera tollit.
Franguntur remi; tum prora avertit et **undis**
dat latus, insequitur cumulo praeruptus aquae mons.
Hi summo in fluctu pendent, his **unda** *dehiscens*
terram inter fluctus aperit, furit aestus **harenis**.
Tris **Notus** *abreptas in saxa latentia torquet*
(saxa vocant Itali mediis quae in fluctibus Aras,
dorsum immane mari summo), tris **Eurus** *ab alto*
in brevia et **Syrtis** *urguet (miserabile visu)*
inliditque vadis atque aggere cingit harenae.
(Verg. *Aen.* 1, 84-86; 102-112)

---

[152] Like Medea, Alcmena also lists the names of places which are familiar to her.
[153] The choice of the myth is, however, a very delicate matter, as we know that Seneca's tragedies have a palimpsestic structure (cf. A. J. Boyle, *Tragic Seneca*..., p. 89). We can only assume that the main inspiration came from the ancestor poet.

Seneca:
[…] *Undique **incumbunt** simul*
rapiuntque pelagus infimo eversum solo
adversus <u>Euro</u> Zephyrus et Boreae <u>Notus</u>.
Sua quisque mittunt tela et infesti fretum
emoliuntur, turbo <u>convolvit mare</u>:
*Strymonius altas **Aquilo** contorquet nives*
*Lybicusque <u>harenas</u> Auster ac **<u>Syrtes</u>** agit,*
*[nec manet in Austro; fit gravis nimbis **Notus**]*[154]
*imbre auget <u>undas</u>; **Eurus** orientem movet*
Nabataea quatiens regna et Eoos sinus.
(*Ag.* 474-483)

Let us now look at the verbal sequences:

Virgil:
incubuere — *<u>Eurusque Notusque</u>* — *<u>volvunt ... fluctus</u>* — **Aquilone** — *<u>undis</u>* — *unda* — *<u>harenis</u>* — ***Notus*** — ***<u>Eurus</u>*** — ***<u>Syrtis</u>***

Seneca:
incumbunt — *<u>Euro ... Notus</u>* — *<u>convolvit mare</u>* — **Aquilo** — *<u>harenas</u>* — ***<u>Syrtes</u>*** — *Notus* — *<u>undas</u>* — ***<u>Eurus</u>***

The sequence, though slightly altered, is clear enough as a message from Seneca to the listener: "Here I'm competing with Virgil — who do you think is better?" Seneca uses all the names of the winds used by Virgil (even adding Zephyrus and Boreas), the name of the *Syrtes* and some other words, so that his Roman audience could easily identify the hypotext and understand the game he was playing with them.

Another messenger speech which I would like to draw attention to is Creo's monologue from *Oedipus* (*Oed.* 530-658). Here Creo relates the scene of the summoning of the ghost of Laius from the underworld. It contains some very clear allusions to the *nekyia* in Virgil's *Aeneid*:

Virgil:
Obvertunt <u>pelago</u> proras; tum dente tenaci
[…]
*Iam subeunt Triviae **lucos** atque aurea tecta.*
[…]
Redditus his primum terris tibi, <u>Phoebe</u>, sacravit
remigium alarum posuitque immania templa.
(Verg. *Aen.* 6, 3, 13, 18-19)

---

[154] Although the editor is not convinced of the authenticity of this line, the name *Notus* which appears here is a strong argument in favour of its authenticity, as the name of the wind is in keeping with the pattern of Senecan *aemulatio* present in this passage.

Seneca:
*Cr. Est procul ab urbe **lucus** ilicibus niger*
[…]
et Paphia myrtus et per immensum mare
motura remos alnus et Phoebo obvia
enode Zephyris pinus opponens latus.
(*Oed.* 530, 539-541)

And here we have the sequences of words:

Virgil:
pelago — **lucos** — Phoebe

Seneca:
lucus — *mare* — Phoebo

It is quite clear that these two passages contain exactly the same motifs (the grove, the sea and the god Phoebus). As this is only the beginning, let us investigate both passages further and look for more traces of *aemulatio*. Here is another passage where Seneca not only uses words which were first used by Virgil, but even preserves the order in which they appear in the *Aeneid*:

Virgil:
Vestibulum ante ipsum primisque in faucibus Orci
***Luctus** et ultrices posuere cubilia Curae;*
pallentesque habitant Morbi tristisque Senectus
*et **Metus** et malesuada Fames ac turpis Egestas,*
terribiles visu formae, Letumque Labosque;
(Verg. *Aen.* 6, 273-277)

Seneca:
Tum torva Erinys sonuit et caecus Furor
Horrorque et una quidquid aeternae creant
*celantque tenebrae: **Luctus** avellens comam*
aegerque lassum sustinens Morbus caput,
*gravis Senectus sibimet et pendens **Metus***
avidumque populi Pestis Ogygii malum —
(*Oed.* 589-594)

Let us look at the sequences:

Virgil:
Luctus — *Morbi* — Senectus — **Metus**

Seneca:
Luctus — *Morbus* — Senectus — **Metus**

Here there can be no doubt that Seneca is emulating Virgil. The sequence is almost unchanged, only *Morbus* being in the singular, while in Virgil it was in the plural.

There is also an interesting parallel between the composition of these two passages:

In the *Aeneid*:
The prophetess **Sibyl** helps Aeneas to find out the truth about the *future* which *is known only by his father, Anchises.*

In *Oedipus*:
The prophet **Tiresias** helps Oedipus to find out the truth about the *past* which *is known only by his father, Laius.*

In the text there are yet more similarities, for example:

Virgil:
At, **Phoebi** *nondum patiens immanis in* antro
bacchatur vates, *magnum si pectore possit*
excussisse deum: tanto magis ille fatigat
os rabidum, *fera corda domans, fingitque premendo.*
(Verg. *Aen.* 6, 77-80)

Seneca:
Tristis sub illa, lucis et **Phoebi** *inscius*
restagnat umor frigore aeterno rigens;
limosa pigrum circumit fontem palus.
Huc ut sacerdos intulit senior gradum,
haut est moratus: * * * *
* * * *praestitit noctem locus.*
Tum effossa tellus, et super rapti rogis
iaciuntur ignes. Ipse funesto integit
vates *amictu corpus et frondem quatit;*
squalente cultu maestus ingreditur senex,
lugubris imos palla perfundit pedes,
mortifera canam taxus adstringit comam.
Nigro bidentes vellere atque atrae boves
antro *trahuntur. Flamma praedatur dapes*
vivumque trepidat igne ferali pecus.
Vocat inde manes teque qui manes regis
et obsidentem claustra Lethaei lacus,
carmenque magicum volvit et **rabido** *minax*
decantat **ore** *quidquid aut placat leves*
aut cogit umbras; sanguinem libat focis
solidasque pecudes urit et multo specum
saturat cruore; libat et niveum insuper
lactis liquorem, [...]
(*Oed.* 545-566).

Here again we have an interesting sequence:

Virgil:
Phoebi — <u>antro</u> — <u>vates</u> — **os rabidum**

Seneca:
Phoebi — <u>vates</u> — <u>antro</u> — **rabido... ore**

Here too Seneca repeats the same words in almost the same order. He merely switches the order of the words *vates* and *antro* and also breaks the expression *os rabidum* into two parts: *rabido minax decantat ore*, forming a sophisticated hyperbaton.

The next passage where Seneca emulates Virgil's *nekyia* is the description of the grove:

Virgil
discolor unde auri per <u>ramos</u> aura refulsit.
Quale solet silvis brumali frigore viscum
*fronde **virere** nova, quod non sua seminat <u>arbos</u>,*
*et croceo fetu teretis circumdare **truncos**,*
talis erat species auri frondentis opaca
ilice, sic leni crepitabat brattea vento.
(Verg. *Aen.* 6, 204-209)

Seneca:
***virente** semper alligat **trunco** nemus,*
curvosque tendit <u>quercus</u> et putres situ
annosa <u>ramos</u>: huius abrupit latus
edax vetustas; illa, iam fessa cadens
radice, fulta pendet aliena trabe.
(*Oed.* 533-537)

And here are the sequences:

Virgil:
<u>ramos</u> — **virere** — <u>arbos</u> — **truncos**

Seneca:
virente — **trunco** — <u>quercus</u> — <u>ramos</u>

A few lines further down there is another place where Seneca quite obviously alludes to Virgil. This is the description of the entrance to the underworld:

Virgil:
*Spelunca alta fuit vastoque **immanis hiatu**,*
scrupea, tuta <u>lacu</u> nigro nemorumque <u>tenebris</u>
(Verg. *Aen.* 6, 237-238).

Seneca:
*Subito dehiscit terra et **immenso sinu**
laxata patuit — ipse pallentes deos
vidi inter umbras, ipse torpentes <u>lacus
noctemque veram</u>*
(*Oed.* 582-585).

The sequences are as follows:

Virgil:
immanis hiatu — <u>lacu</u> — <u>tenebris</u>

Seneca:
immenso sinu — <u>lacus</u> — <u>noctemque veram</u>

Most interesting of all, however, is the moment when the world of the living meets that of the dead. Virgil's *nekyia* is a classical, Homeric κατάβασις in the literal meaning: Aeneas and Sybill *go down* to the underworld. Seneca's *nekyia* is different — the dead *come up* to the earth:

Virgil:
*Ibant **obscuri** sola sub nocte per <u>umbram</u>
perque domos Ditis vacuas et inania regna:*
(Verg. *Aen.* 6, 268-269)

Seneca:
*Pavide **latebras** nemoris <u>umbrosi</u> petunt
animae trementes:* [...]
(*Oed.* 608-609)

We have seen this strategy before — in *Medea* and in *Troades*. Seneca takes a motif from his epic predecessor and then inverts it. Here he takes the classical motif of κατάβασις (*going down*) and changes it to *coming up*, so that instead of depicting a living person going down to the underworld he depicts the dead emerging from Hades.

Instead of presenting this scene directly,[155] Seneca decided to introduce an epic *nekyia* that would compete with the most famous *nekyia* in Roman literature. Indeed, not only did he challenge Virgil, but he also turned Virgil's motif upside down.[156]

---

[155] In Greek tragedy ghosts usually appear directly as normal *dramatis personae*, e.g. Aeschylus' Darius (Aesch. *Pers.* 681 ff.) and Clytemnestra (Aesch. *Choe.* 94 ff.) or Euripides' Polydorus (Eur. *Hec.* 1 ff.).

[156] Oh the infernal motifs in all Senecan tragedies see: P. Mantovanelli, *Populus infernae Stygis*, passim.

The *Nekyia* is a typical epic motif and its presence in Seneca's *Oedipus* is a formal innovation.[157] It is a very good example of the so-called *Kreuzung der Gattungen* which Seneca pursued to such an extent that he incorporated whole compositional elements characteristic of epic poetry into the structure of his tragedies.

Seneca's *nekyia*, however, is different from that of his model. Virgil's version is much more cheerful, as — besides some powerful images of Hades — it also contains descriptions of the brighter parts of the underworld.[158] By contrast, Seneca shows only its darkest and gloomiest face. *Oedipus* abounds in *verba timendi*,[159] as it is a tragedy of unabated tension and terror.

One of Seneca's favourite techniques is highly detailed description, especially in scenes of cruelty and terror. An example is the final messenger speech in *Oedipus*, which is an account of how Oedipus blinds himself:

> **Scrutatur** *avidus manibus uncis* <u>lumina</u>,
> *radice ab ima funditus vulsos simul*
> *evolvit orbes; haeret in vacuo manus*
> *et fixa penitus* <u>unguibus</u> *lacerat cavos*
> *alte recessus luminum et inanes sinus*
> *saevitque frustra plusque quam satis est furit.*
> (*Oed.* 965-970).

This scene was later imitated by Seneca's nephew Lucan in a similarly terrifying scene, where the witch Erichtho attempts to resuscitate the corpse of a soldier:[160]

> *Continuo fugere lupi, fugere revolsis*
> <u>unguibus</u> *inpastae volucres, dum Thessala vatem*
> *eligit et gelidas leto* **scrutata** <u>medullas</u>
> *pulmonis rigidi stantis sine volnere fibras*
> *invenit et vocem defuncto in corpore quaerit.*
> (Luc. *Phars.* 6, 627-631)

---

[157] *Longissimam (v. 530-623) quae est de Lai mortui specie ab inferis excitanda, ἔκφρασιν hoc solummodo consilio in fabulam inclusam esse causa in hoc posita est, quod ea materia ut dinosi fucaretur, aptissima Senecae est visa. Creon primum locum, deinde quomodo Tiresias sacra curaverit, post quemadmodum mortuorum umbrae advocatae sint, tum ad extremum Tartari atque eius deorum ostentorumque atrocitatem quae notis iam verbis in maius extollitur, evidenter describit.* (J. Smereka, *op. cit.*, p. 624).

[158] Cf. F. Solmsen, *The World of the Dead in Book 6 of the "Aeneid"*, [in:] *Oxford Readings in Vergil's "Aeneid"*, ed. by J. Harrison, Oxford 1990, p. 215.

[159] Cf. P. Mantovanelli, *El Hado, la casualidad, el reino...*, pp. 238-239.

[160] Lucan's technique of imitation (which is surprisingly similar to that of Seneca) has already been analysed by scholars (cf. J. Masters, *Poetry and Civil War in Lucan's "Bellum Civile"*, Cambridge 1992, pp. 26, 123-124).

And here are the sequences:

Seneca:
***scrutatur** — lumina — unguibus*

Lucan:
*unguibus — **scrutata** — medullas*

As we can see, Lucan takes Seneca's motif (leaving a verbal sequence, as Seneca used to) and makes it even more horrifying: Oedipus plunges his fingers into his own eyes, while the witch plunges both hands into a corpse, looking for tissues that have not yet decomposed.

The final messenger speech in *Oedipus*, as well as its Lucanian imitation, is very graphic, so that the listener or reader can easily imagine all the details of the dreadful deed. As Seneca does with Ovid, Lucan emulates a passage of his uncle's tragedy which contains a similar motif (hands penetrating into human flesh) and renders it even more macabre.

As we have seen, Ovid imitated Latro, Seneca imitated Ovid and eventually Lucan imitated Seneca. Ovid only copied those passages whose style and rhetorical πάθος he liked best, while Seneca in the main copied those which exhibited some strong aesthetic qualities.

There is one more place which deserves our attention. This is the prologue of *Thyestes* which, as scholars have already noted,[161] alludes to one particular scene in Virgil's *Aeneid* (7, 447-457). Let us look at both passages:

Virgil:
Talibus Allecto dictis exarsit in iras.
At iuveni oranti subitus tremor occupat artus,
deriguere oculi: tot Erinys sibilat hydris
*tantaque se facies aperit; tum flammea **torquens***
lumina cunctantem et quaerentem dicere plura
reppulit, et geminos erexit crinibus anguis,
verberaque insonuit rabidoque haec addidit ore:
"en ego victa situ, quam veri effeta senectus
arma inter regum falsa formidine ludit;
respice ad haec: adsum dirarum ab sede sororum,
bella manu letumque gero."
Sic effata facem iuveni coniecit et atro
lumine fumantis fixit sub pectore taedas.
(Verg. *Aen.* 7, 445-457)

Seneca:
[...] *Fu. Ante perturba domum*

---

[161] Cf. M. Braginton, *op. cit.*, p. 51; cf. Seneca, *Thyestes*, pp. 85-86, 102; cf. A. Schiesaro, *op. cit.*, p. 34 ff.; cf. P. Mantovanelli, *Il prologo del "Tieste"...*, p. 203.

inferque tecum proelia et ferri malum
regibus amorem, concute insano ferum
pectus tumultu. Ta. [...]
[...]
*Quid ora terres verbere et **tortos** ferox*
minaris <u>angues</u>? quid famem infixam intimis
agitas medullis? flagrat incensum siti
cor et perustis flamma visceribus micat.
sequor.
Fu: Hunc, hunc furorem divide in totam domum.
(*Thy.* 83-86; 96-101)

Although this time Seneca uses only two words which may (or may not) have been taken from Virgil, they might well have sufficed as a stylistic hint for contemporary literati to enable them to spot the *aemulatio*:

Virgil:
torquens — <u>*anguis*</u>

Seneca:
tortos — <u>*angues*</u>

Whereas in the *Aeneid* the Fury Allecto incites Turnus to take revenge on the Trojans, in *Thyestes* the Fury incites the dead Tantalus to infect the palace of Atreus with the spirit of his own crime. In Virgil's version the scene is partly related by the narrator and partly "acted out" by the characters. In Seneca there is a scene in pure dialogue. Here then we have a case where the epic poet applies dramatic means to epic, while the dramatic poet — borrowing and transforming the Virgilian motif of a Fury inciting someone to do evil — remains faithful to the dramatic form.

In Virgil's version it is the narrator who informs us about the way in which the Fury talks to Turnus (*verberaque insonuit rabidoque haec addidit ore:* ...). In Seneca's version it is Tantalus himself who informs the listener or reader about the Fury's method of exerting pressure (*ora terres verbere, minaris angues, famem ... agitas*).

Here again we can easily see the transformation of a motif which has been "borrowed" from Virgil. Seneca takes a similar pattern (a Fury inciting a character to do something evil) and transforms it into something much more expressive: instead of a young Italian king we have an infernal spectre; instead of revenge for betrayed love and a betrayed political alliance we have a veritable plague of evil.

Seneca has exaggerated every element of the Virgilian pattern. He also uses a highly original technique: with the sudden appearance of the Fury, Tantalus' monologue becomes a dialogue.[162] Moreover, neither participant of this peculiar dialogue belongs to the world of the living.[163]

---

[162] Cf. E. Wesołowska, *Prologi tragedii Seneki*, p. 81.
[163] Cf. *ibidem*.

The exaggeration is therefore even greater: instead of a metaphorical scene (in Virgil the Fury impersonates Turnus' state of mind) Seneca composes a fantastic[164] scene with an infernal nightmare. This is a very good example of sophisticated literary *aemulatio* which is accompanied by a total aesthetic change.

At the end of this chapter let us now briefly look at the composition of the *Phoenissae*. This play is particularly interesting because it is unfinished and has been left without the choruses, which Seneca would probably have added in later, after finishing the dialogues.[165] He was not yet ready to dispense with the choruses altogether because in his day they were still an indispensable part of any tragedy.[166]

Let us look at the structure of this play:

DIALOGUE I:
Oedipus   (w. 1-50)
Antigone   (w. 51-79)
Oedipus   (w. 80-181)
Antigone   (w. 182-215)
Oedipus   (w. 216-287)
Antigone   (w. 288-294)
Oedipus   (w. 295-319)

DIALOGUE II:
Nuntius   (w. 320-327)
Oedipus   (w. 328-347)
Nuntius   (w. 347-349)
Oedipus   (w. 350-362)

DIALOGUE III:
Iocasta   (w. 363-386)
Satelles   (w. 387-402)
Antigone   (w. 403-406)
Iocasta   (w. 407-418)
Satelles   (w. 419)
Iocasta   (w. 420-426)
Satelles   (w. 427-442)

DIALOGUE IV:
Iocasta   (w. 443-477)
Polynices   (w. 478-480)
Iocasta   (w. 480-585)
Polynices   (w. 586-598)
Iocasta   (w. 599-643)
Polynices   (w. 643-644)
Iocasta   (w. 645-651)

---

[164] Cf. *ibidem*, p. 79.
[165] Cf. R. Mayer, *op. cit.*, p. 35.
[166] Cf. *ibidem*.

DIALOGUE V: (unfinished?)
Eteocles   (w. 651-653)
Iocasta   (w. 653)
Eteocles   (w. 654-659)
Iocasta   (w. 660)
Eteocles   (w. 661-662)
Iocasta   (w. 663)
Eteocles   (w. 664)

As we can see, this play also lacks prologues, which may indicate that they too were to be added in later. If we treated the first dialogue as a prologue, it would last for half of the play, which would make little sense.

One interesting thing about this play are the long monologues.[167] The longest of them is 101 lines long. This is the monologue in which Oedipus considers committing suicide and confides his plan to his daughter Antigone. Although this monologue — as far as its structure is concerned — obviously owes much to Sophocles[168] and Euripides,[169] it is also very strongly linked to Virgil.

The motif of considering suicide in the presence of another person seems familiar: it has already appeared in the *Aeneid* in the scene where Dido confides her desperate plan to her sister Anna:

Virgil:
Tum breviter Barcen nutricem adfata Sychaei,
namque suam patria antiqua cinis ater habebat:
"Annam, cara mihi nutrix, huc siste sororem;
dic corpus properet fluviali spargere lympha
et pecudes secum et monstrata piacula ducat.
Sic veniat tuque ipsa pia tege tempora vitta.
Sacra Iovi Stygio, quae rite incepta paravi,
perficere est animus finemque imponere curis
Dardaniique rogum capitis permittere flammae."
Sic ait. Illa gradum studio celerabat anili.
At trepida et coeptis immanibus effera Dido,
sanguineam volvens aciem maculisque trementis
interfusa genas et pallida morte futura,
interiora domus inrumpit limina et **altos**
<u>*conscendit* furibunda **rogos** *ensemque*</u> *recludit*

---

[167] *It is certainly true that the influence of Seneca's declamatory background is strong, too strong at times for the good of the drama. Static monologues of great length abound, dialogue is almost exclusively confined to point-scoring in stichomythic exchanges, and the self-conscious striving for effect* [...]. (Seneca, *Phoenissae*, ed. with an introd and comm. by M. Frank, Leiden 1995, p. 32). In my opinion it was not only rhetoric which influenced Senecan tragedy in this way, but above all epic poetry.

[168] Cf. *ibidem*, p. 17 ff.
[169] Cf. *ibidem*, p. 21 ff.

Dardanium, non hos quaesitum munus in usus.
(Verg. Aen. 4, 632-647)

Seneca:
Desiste coepto, virgo: ius vitae ac necis
meae penes me est. Regna deserui libens,
regnum mei retineo. Si fida es comes,
*<u>ensem</u> parenti trade, sed **notum nece**_*
*ensem **paterna**. Tradis? An gnati tenent*
cum regno et illum? Faciet, ubicumque est, opus.
Ibi sit; relinquo. Natus hunc habeat meus,
sed uterque. — Flammas potius et vastum aggerem
*compone; in **altos** <u>ipse me immittam</u> **rogos**_*
[haerebo ad ignes, funebrem escendam struem]
pectusque solvam durum et in cinerem dabo
hoc quidquid in me vivit. — Ubi saevum est mare?
(*Phoe.* 103-114).

As in previous "common places", here too Seneca has left us a clue in the form of a verbal sequence:

Virgil:
altos — <u>conscendit</u> — **rogos** — <u>ensemque</u> — **Dardanium**

Seneca:
<u>ensem</u> — **notum nece** — <u>ensem</u>[170] — **paterna** — in **altos** — <u>ipse me immittam</u> — **rogos**

Let us look at the general pattern of the motif:
1. Dido talks to Anna — her sister and only friend.
   Oedipus talks to Antigone — his daughter and only friend.
2. Dido is planning to commit suicide and tells Anna.
   Oedipus is planning to commit suicide and tells Antigone.
3. Dido kills herself with the sword given to her by Aeneas.
   Oedipus wants to kill himself with the sword with which he killed his father.
4. Dido ascends the pyre herself.
   Oedipus wants to ascend the pyre himself.
5. Dido dies.
   Oedipus does not die.

Seneca has created a story line parallel to the Virgilian one, but there is a difference between them: Dido really does commit suicide whereas Oedipus does not. It

---

[170] The word *ensis*, repeated twice, has already been seen as a borrowing from Virgil, but from elsewhere: *Hirschberg* [...] *observes that "notus ensis" is a Vergilian expression, citing Verg. Aen. 12.759 "nomine quemque vocans notumque efflagitat ensem"*. (*Ibidem*, p. 109).

seems, therefore, that Seneca has included this passage merely in order to emulate Virgil, as he follows all the elements of Virgil's pattern but in the end the character does not carry out his plan.[171] We may even suspect that Oedipus' suicidal thoughts are merely a good pretext to emulate a masterful passage of Virgil's poem.

Oedipus has his second long monologue when he is leaving Thebes. Its beginning is very similar to the beginning of the tale of Nyktimene in Ovid's *Metamorphoses*:

Ovid:
*An, quae per totam res est notissima Lesbon,
non audita tibi est, patrium temerasse cubile
Nyctimenen? Avis illa quidem, sed **conscia culpae**
<u>conspectum lucemque fugit</u> tenebrisque pudorem
celat et a cunctis expellitur aethere toto.*
(Ovid. *Met*. 2, 591-595)

Seneca:
*Oe. Me <u>fugio, fugio</u> **conscium scelerum omnium**
pectus, manumque hanc <u>fugio</u> et <u>hoc caelum</u> et <u>deos</u>
et <u>dira fugio scelera</u> quae feci innocens.*
(*Phoe*. 216-218)

Now let us look at the verbal sequence:

Ovid:
consica culpae — <u>*conspectum lucemque*</u> — <u>*fugit*</u>

Seneca:
<u>*fugio, fugio*</u> — ***conscium scelerum omnium*** — <u>*fugio*</u> — <u>*hoc caelum*</u> — <u>*deos*</u> — <u>*dira*</u> — <u>*fugio*</u> — <u>*scelera*</u>

This sequence shows us how Seneca makes the Ovidian version more expressive. He changes the noun *culpa* to *scelera omnia*. Nyktimene runs away from light (*conspectum lucemque*), but Oedipus runs away from his own heart, his hand, his country, the gods and his own crime (*conscium scelerum omnium pectus, manumque hanc fugio et hoc caelum et deos et dira fugio scelera*).

Here too Seneca emulates a passage from another poet's work with a similar pattern:
1. Nyktimene is guilty of incest with her own father.
   Oedipus is guilty of incest with his own mother
2. Nyktimene is conscious of her guilt.
   Oedipus is conscious of his guilt.
3. Nyktimene, having changed into an owl, dreads daylight.
   Oedipus, having blinded himself, cannot see the daylight.

---

[171] Scholars have noted that the first act of *Phoenissae* is also strongly influenced by rhetoric: *In* Phoen., *the influence of declamation is easily discernible. The first act (1-319), in which Antigone urges Oedipus not to commit suicide, is a* suasoria *in a cramatic form* [...]. (*Ibidem*, p. 32).

4. Nyktimene is an exile (... fugit; ... expellitur ...).
   Oedipus is an exile (me fugio, fugio ...; ... fugio ...; ... fugio ...)

This monologue is very interesting because it contains a quasi-epic narration of the life of Oedipus (*Oed.* 243 ff.). Oedipus is therefore both the narrator and the hero of the story he tells, whereas Ovid's Nyktimene is only the hero, watched over by a transparent narrator.

Oedipus recounts the events of his life in the form of an epic narration, but from his own point of view as one of the *dramatis personae*. Unlike Medea, he keeps to the chronological order of events, beginning with his childhood (*infanti quoque decreta mors est*, v. 244) and ending with the present situation and the war between his two sons (*hic occupato cedere imperio negat/ ... ille... / ... et Argos exul atque urbes movet/ Graias in arma*, vv. 281-284).

In *Oedipus* there are two messengers: Nuntius and Satelles, but they hardly say anything. Their speeches are not traditional, long messenger speeches, but are confined to a few lines and the characters could well do without their help. In *Agamemnon* there is also a similarly unimportant messenger whose extremely short speech, consisting of five lines (vv. 392-396), is totally insignificant.[172] In both cases there is simply no need for major messenger speeches, as all past and present events are related by the characters themselves.

As we can see, Seneca's tragedies combine the features of drama (formally and metrically) with those of epic poetry (practically). They consist mainly of narratives and descriptions, but there is no traditional narrator, for the narration is divided up among the characters who tell their own stories from their own individual points of view.

It is of course not true to say that in a drama there is no place for major narratives or descriptions. In Seneca's plays, however, these structures dominate the dynamic interactions between the characters.[173] They are also the major constituent of the composition of Seneca's tragedies.

As we have seen in this chapter, Seneca was a master of *aemulatio*. His father — Seneca the Elder — has left an excellent vivisection of the practice of quoting another author's works in altered form, which was a favourite pastime of ancient poets such as Ovid. Seneca turned this practice into a literary contest with his two great rivals — Ovid and Virgil — both of whom he regarded as his *ancestral poets*.

The aim of this chapter has been to demonstrate to what extent Seneca depended on his major models — Virgil and Ovid — and by what criteria he alluded to their original works. The analysis of certain passages of his tragedies has shown that he alluded to them in two ways: by retelling the myths already told by them (e.g. the myth of Medea), or by repeating the motifs they had used or invented (e.g. the motif of the audience).

---

[172] Cf. Seneca, *Agamemnon*, p. 398.
[173] Cf. idem, *Phoenissae*, p. 32.

CHAPTER III

Contrariis in contraria agitur[174]
The Contrast Technique

Omnia postremo bona sensibus et mala tactu
dissimili inter se pugnant perfecta figura

Lucretius, *De rerum natura*[175]

In the previous chapters of this book I have mainly investigated the formal and genological aspects of Seneca's tragedies, concentrating on their highly narrative and descriptive character, which likens them somewhat to epic poetry. I have also drawn an analogy between some passages of Seneca's plays and corresponding passages of his epic ancestors — Virgil and Ovid.

In this chapter I will examine the stylistic and aesthetic features of these tragedies in order to show how Seneca influenced his audience's emotions and stimulated their imaginations. I will begin by analysing his peculiar technique of juxtaposing opposite meanings,[176] which I have called "the contrast technique". This technique plays an important role above all in those places where a hero dies or something dreadful happens. These parts of the play are specially designed to arouse terror or anxiety, so here Seneca uses the most powerful language possible.

We must remember that Seneca did not write for *us*, but for his contemporaries, who had very powerful imaginations and a fondness for the cruel and savage.

---

[174] *De clem.* 1, 12.
[175] Lucr. *De rer. nat.* 2, 408-409.
[176] Scholars have noted that there are many contrasts in Seneca's tragedies: *Yet, far from laying bare the "rhetorical" nature of Senecan tragedy, frames underline the most profoundly dramatic aspects of the play. Frames define boundaries and thus mark separation and even detachment, but precipitate comparison and contrast. They dissect different parts of the play, but they hardly arrange an orderly, inert sequence of tableaux; on the contrary, they highlight the inevitable collision of dramatic levels and the relentless conflicts that plague successive generations.* (A. Schiesaro, *op. cit.*, p. 64). It would seem, however, that to date no one has forcefully argued that Seneca's use of contrasts is the result of a consistent literary strategy.

Nero's times were times of luxury, exuberance and cruelty and there was little room for idyllic beauty,[177]

In this period a powerful work of art meant one that was made up entirely of negative aesthetic qualities. Disharmony was then the main constituent of an aesthetic experience.[178] The pursuit of strong sensations and a longing for the sublime had become a serious challenge for any artist, and especially for a poet.

Looking for a means of vivid expression in order to achieve the most powerful effects, Seneca did not concentrate on the moral aspects of myths (as did Sophocles) nor on their political aspects (as did Virgil). Instead, he made a point of choosing the darkest and most incredible elements of the ancient stories and developed them into powerful literary images.

The main entertainment in Nero's Rome were spectacles of death. Nero was not the only emperor who took pleasure in watching them, however. We learn from Suetonius that Claudius also delighted in watching the faces of dying gladiators:

Quocumque gladiatorio munere, vel suo vel alieno, etiam forte prolapsos iugulari iubebat, maxime retiarios, ut expirantium facies videret. (Suet. *Claud.* 34, 2).

Seneca describes the cruelty which was ubiquitous in imperial Rome:

Non privatim solum sed publice furimus. Homicidia compescimus et singulas caedes: quid bella et occisarum gentium gloriosum scelus? Non avaritia, non crudelitas modum novit. (*Epist.* 95, 30).

He also mentions gladiators who decide to commit suicide rather than go into the arena:

Nuper in ludo bestiariorum unus e Germanis, cum ad matutina spectacula pararetur, secessit ad exonerandum corpus: nullum aliud illi dabatur sine custode secretum: ibi lignum id, quod ad emundanda obscena adhaerente spongia positum est, totum in gulam farsit et interclusis faucibus spiritum elisit. Hoc fuit morti contumeliam facere. Ita prorsus, parum munde et parum decenter: quid est stultius quam fastidiose mori? O virum fortem, o dignum cui fati daretur electio! Quam fortiter ille gladio usus esset, quam animose in profundam se altitudinem maris aut abscisae rupis immisisset! Undique destitutus invenit quemadmodum et mortem sibi deberet et telum, ut scias ad moriendum nihil aliud in mora esse quam velle. Existimetur de facto hominis acerrimi, ut cuique visum erit, dum hoc constet, praeferendam esse spurcissimam mortem servituti mundissimae. Quoniam coepi sordidis exemplis uti, perseverabo: plus enim a se quisque exiget, si viderit hanc rem etiam a contemptissimis posse contemni. Catones Scipionesque et alios, quos audire cum admiratione consuevimus, supra imitationem positos putamus:

---

[177] *Seneca's tragedies thus seem to be the artistic expressions of a clever, yet deeply brooding mind trapped in the sophisticated but violent society of Neronian Rome.* (D. Mastronarde, *op. cit.*, p. 315).

[178] Cf. M. Wallis, *op. cit.*, p. 199.

iam ego istam virtutem habere tam multa exempla in ludo bestiario quam in ducibus belli civilis ostendam. Cum adveheretur nuper inter custodias quidam ad matutinum spectaculum missus, tamquam somno premente nutaret, caput usque eo demisit, donec radiis insereret, et tamdiu se in sedili suo tenuit donec cervicem circumactu rotae frangeret: eodem vehiculo, quo ad poenam ferebatur, effugit. (Epist. 70, 20-23)

The tremendous popularity of the *ludi* can be explained in the following way: the game was founded on pairs of opposites such as life and death, security and insecurity, power and helplessness.[179] These produce feelings similar to terror, and so of the sublime.[180]

It seems that Seneca's contemporaries were as eager to experience the sublime as were the contemporaries of Edmund Burke, whose mentality and taste changed for ever after the horrors of the French Revolution. Similarly, the atmosphere of terror and insecurity during the reign of two mad emperors — Caligula and Nero — changed the mentality as well as the taste of the Romans.[181]

The times of Seneca, however, were the golden age of the amphitheatre. Watching death and mutilation from a safe distance, his contemporaries experienced the sublime in its purest form.[182] From our point of view it was both cruel and primitive, but from their point of view it was simply a normal pastime — much like watching films nowadays.

The reason why the ancient Romans became so excited at the sight of dying men and mutilated corpses seems to be that they found it extremely frightening — and an ugly object which excites a strong feeling of terror is sublime.[183]

Ugliness is the exact opposite of beauty, but Seneca very often juxtaposes the two in a strong contrast. The following passage describing the death of Hippolytus is perhaps the best example of the use of this technique:

Late cruentat arva et inlisum caput
scopulis* resultat; auferunt dumi comas,*
et ora durus pulcra populatur lapis
peritque multo vulnere infelix decor.
(Phae. 1093-1096)

Seneca's nephew Lucan imitates this passage in the scene where the witch Erichtho drags the corpse of a dead soldier towards her cave:

---

[179] Cf. P. Plass, *op. cit.*, p. 25.
[180] *Whatever is fitted in any sort to excite the ideas of pain, and danger, that is to say, whatever is in any sort terrible, or is conversant about terrible objects, or operates in a manner analogous to terror, is a source of the sublime.* (E. Burke, *op. cit.*, p. 86).
[181] Cf. A. Futrell, *Blood in the Arena...*, pp. 48-49.
[182] Cf. E. Burke, *op. cit.*, p. 163.
[183] *Ugliness I imagine likewise to be consistent enough with an idea of the sublime. But I would by no means insinuate that ugliness of itself is a sublime idea, unless united with such qualities as excite a strong terror. (Ibidem, p. 153).* Cf. M. Wallis, *op. cit.*, pp. 28-38.

*Electum tandem traiecto gutture corpus
ducit, et inserto laqueis feralibus unco*
per scopulos *miserum trahitur, per saxa cadaver
victurum montisque cavi, quem tristis Erictho
damnarat sacris, alta sub rupe locatur.*
(Luc. *Phars.* 6, 637-641)

What is interesting is that Lucan has left a verbal sequence, marking the literary allusion:

Seneca:
scopulis — *resultat* — *lapis*

Lucan:
per scopulos — *trahitur* — *per saxa*

Beauty becomes *infelix decor*,[184] as triumphant ugliness[185] destroys it. The destruction of the face of Hippolytus may also be interpreted in moral terms, as a symbol of the destruction of moral innocence by the forces of evil. The man's physical beauty is the equivalent of his moral rectitude, while his horrible death is the equivalent of Phaedra's slander.[186]

The shocking image of ugliness which ruthlessly conquers beauty is productive of the sublime, as these two aesthetic qualities are juxtaposed in a strong contrast.[187] The more handsome the face of the hero, the more horrible is its disfigurement. The more vivid this contrast is, the more powerful is the effect of the image.

This passage is very typical of Seneca. The contrast arises from the juxtaposition of two elements: positive and negative. The latter defeats and destroys the former. The basis of all these contrasts is the primary contrast between good and evil.

The evil element being more powerful, Seneca always lays greater stress on it, as in the passage from *Phaedra* quoted above. Let us look at the structure of line 1095:

ora — **durus** — *pulcra* — *populatur* — **lapis**.

---

[184] *It was the beauty of Hippolytus which attracted Phaedra, so the curse operates against it chiefly.* (Seneca, *Phaedra*, p. 183).

[185] *The cult of ugliness is the price this kind of drama* [i.e. stoic drama] *has to pay, and pays gladly, for its fixation upon the hero's selfconsciousness.* (T. Rosenmeyer, *Senecan Drama and Stoic Cosmology*, Berkeley 1989, p. 57). On the continuation of this aesthetic see: R. S. Miola, *Shakespeare and Classical Tragedy. The Influence of Seneca*, Oxford 1992, p. 12.

[186] The moral context of Seneca's tragedies has, of course, nothing in common with moralizing — it is simply a reflection of his philosophical interests.

[187] In an interesting article D. Henry and B. Walker have noted that the entire plot of *Phaedra* is built on the contrast between two worlds: Phaedra (the realm of "phantasmagoria" and chaos) and Hippolytus (the realm of "idyll" and order): *Antithetical though the two worlds of phantasmagoria and idyll are, their separation is not complete.* (*op. cit.*, p. 234).

There is a striking contrast between the expressions *ora pulcra* and *durus lapis*. The words *ora* and *lapis* form the external framework of the line. In the middle is the adjective *pulcra* which stands between the words *durus* and *populatur.* In effect, the smooth face of Hippolytus stands in opposition to the rough rock. The order of all the elements of this line renders the contrast as sharp as possible, therefore making it even more powerful as a source of the sublime.

Seneca uses the contrast technique not only in poetry, but also in prose.[188] The following passage from his *De ira* is a good example of this strategy:

Quid clementia remissius, quid crudelitate negotiosius? (*De ira* 2, 13)

Crudelitas is the exact opposite of *clementia*, as ugliness is the exact opposite of beauty. By juxtaposing the two opposites Seneca has achieved the effect of a strong contrast which in a philosophical work produces the effect of clear reasoning, while in a poem it produces the effect of vividness and strength of artistic expression.

The famous treatise *De clementia* has an antithetic composition founded on the contrast between *clementia* and *crudelitas*. Seneca juxtaposes examples of the former with examples of the latter in order to make the differences between them more obvious. At the beginning he places the image of a bad and cruel emperor alongside that of a good and benevolent one:

Contrariis in contraria agitur; nam cum invisus sit, quia timetur, timeri vult, quia invisus est, et illo execrabili versu, qui multos praecipites dedit, utitur: "Oderint, dum metuant" [Acc. Atr. 31, p. 203], *ignarus, quanta rabies oriatur, ubi supra modum odia creverunt. Temperatus enim timor cohibet animos, adsiduus vero et acer et extrema admovens in audaciam iacentes excitat et omnia experiri suadet* [...]. *Placido tranquilloque regi fida sunt auxilia sua, ut quibus ad communem salutem utatur, gloriosusque miles (publicae enim securitati se dare operam videt) omnem laborem libens patitur ut parentis custos* [...]. (*De clem.* 1, 12-13)

The strongest of all contrasts, however, is that between life and death.[189] This contrast is the key to understanding the social and psychological phenomenon of the Roman games. In Seneca's tragedies it is extremely strong. One of the best examples of this technique is the scene of Polyxena's death:

[...] *Ipsa deiectos gerit*
vultus pudore, sed tamen fulgent genae
magisque solito splendet extremus decor,
[...]

---

[188] Cf. A. Traina, *Lo stile drammatico del filosofo Seneca*, Bologna 1974, pp. 30-31, 88, 93, 111, 113.

[189] Scholars have noted that he perceives death as a phenomenon complementary to life (cf. E. Wesołowska, *Seneki i Marka Aureliusza* ars moriendi, "Studia Classica et Neolatina" 1998, 3, p. 175).

Audax virago non tulit retro gradum;
conversa ad ictum stat truci vultu ferox.
Tam fortis animus omnium mentes ferit,
novumque monstrum est Pyrrhus ad caedem piger.
Ut dextra ferrum penitus exactum abdidit,
subitus recepta morte prorupit cruor
per vulnus ingens. Nec tamen moriens adhuc
deponit animos: cecidit, ut Achilli gravem
factura terram, prona et irato impetu.
(*Tro.* 1137-1139, 1151-1159)

Polyxena's beauty and vital energy are juxtaposed with the invincible power of death.[190] She is executed in public, as were Roman criminals. One moment the princess is a living person with amazing mental strength and the next she becomes a lifeless corpse which slumps to the ground.

Another contrast — which is perhaps Seneca's favourite — is that between light and darkness. Like Caravaggio, he was a master of playing with light. The best example of the use of this contrast is *Thyestes*, which is shot through with the motif of light and darkness. In the prologue itself the ghost of Tantalus recalls Tityos, whose liver grows at night, only to be eaten by a hungry vulture during the day:

[...]
aut poena Tityi qui specu vasto patens
vulneribus atras pascit effossis aves
et nocte reparans quidquid amisit die
plenum recenti pabulum monstro iacet?
(*Thy.* 9-12)[191]

In this passage night is not a time of revival, but one of suffering, as the liver grows back only to cause Tityos more pain.

The banquet scene in *Thyestes* has been recognized by scholars as being highly expressive and — when performed — dramatically powerful:[192]

---

[190] *The extended simile at 1140-2 foregrounds the "perverse" reaction of the crowd to Polyxena's beauty, even as the reference to natural events tries to downplay the disruptive potential of the pleasurable association between imminent death and moving beauty [...]. Such an implication, moreover, is clearly brought out after the simile, as the messenger confirms that Polyxena's beauty stirs strong emotions in the beholders and — for the second time — reinforces the association between aesthetic pleasure and the awareness of a cruel, imminent death.* (A. Schiesaro, *op. cit.*, p. 242).

[191] On the myth of Tityos in Ovid see: P. Mantovanelli, "*Populus infernae Stygis*"..., p. 138.

[192] *The theatricality of the scene is increased by the contrast between darkness outside and light and colour indoors [...]. This is a strongly visual effect, which would work powerfully in the theatre.* (J. Fitch, *op. cit.*, p. 3).

Utinam quidem tenere fugientes deos
possem, et coactos trahere ut ultricem dapem,
omnes viderent — quod sat est, videat pater.
Etiam die nolente discutiam tibi
tenebras, miseriae sub quibus latitant tuae.[193]
Nimis diu conviva securo iaces
hilarique vultu; iam satis mensis datum est
satisque Baccho: sobrio tanta ad mala
opus est Thyeste — Turba famularis, fores
templi relaxa, festa patefiat domus.
Libet videre, capita natorum intuens
quos det colores, verba quae primus dolor
effundat aut ut spiritu expulso stupens
corpus rigescat. Fructus hic operis mei est.
Miserum videre nolo, sed dum fit miser.
Aperta multa tecta conlucent face.
Resupinus ipse purpurae atque auro incubat,
vino gravatum fulciens laeva caput.
Eructat. O me caelitum excelsissimum,
regumque regem! Vota transcendi mea.
(*Thy.* 893-912)

In line 908 great emphasis is laid on the strong light which reveals the horror of the scene (*aperta ... tecta*).[194] There is a strong contrast between an open, illuminated palace and the total darkness surrounding it.

The expression *aperta tecta* would also correspond to the meaning of the previous lines, where Atreus wishes that the fall of Thyestes be visible — "open" — to all the universe (*coactos trahere ut ultricem dapem / omnes viderent*). The opening of the palace to the world means the revelation of Thyestes' terrible punishment.

Later, the light begins to grow faint when Atreus offers Thyestes a goblet of wine:

Vix lucet ignis; ipse quin aether gravis
inter diem noctemque desertus stupet.
Quid hoc? magis magisque concussi labant
convexa caeli; spissior densis coit
caligo tenebris noxque se in noctem abdidit:
fugit omne sidus [...].[195]
(*Thy.* 990-995)

---

[193] discutiam ... tuae: *dispelling darkness usually connotes a return to normal [...], but here darkness is a protection and clarity brings ruin; a similar inversion of the norm underlines HF 50 vidi nocte discussa infernum.* (Seneca, *Thyestes*, p. 218).

[194] aperta ... face = *abAcB* [...]; *the symmetrical arrangement could reflect Atreus' pleasure at the smooth working of his plan. Multa ... face: collective singular, heightening the artifice of the line.* (*Ibidem*, p. 219).

[195] Cf. *ibidem*, p. 228.

There is an extremely strong contrast between the previous illumination and the present darkness. The deep night which overcomes light is a symbol of omnipotent evil, which defeats and consumes all goodness.

The *lux / tenebrae* contrast also appears in other Senecan tragedies, for example in the prologue of his *Agamemnon* (which, let us note, is told by Thyestes himself): *gnatis nepotes miscui-nocti diem* (*Ag.* 36). The motif appears again in Eurybates' account of a sea tempest which takes the Greeks by surprise:

Premunt tenebrae lumina et dirae Stygis
inferna nox est. [...]
(*Ag.* 493-494)

In *Hercules Oetaeus* there is also a passage where darkness conquers light:

"Hoc nulla lux conspiciat, hoc tenebrae tegant
tantum remotae: sic potens vires suas
sanguis tenebit." Verba deprendit quies
mortemque lassis intulit membris sopor.
(*HerO.* 531-534)

Here the contrast is also a symbol. These words are the words of the dying Nessus to Deianira. The evil centaur deceives her in order to destroy Hercules. He advises her to keep his venomous blood in darkness so that it can retain its destructive power.[196]

Later on in the play, as Hercules begins to suffer and his body begins to decay, other contrasts are brought into play — those between life and death and between beauty and ugliness:

Defecit ingens corpus et pesti satis
Herculea non sunt membra — pro, quantum est malum
quod esse vastum fateor, o dirum nefas!
(*HerO.* 1230-1232)

The motif of light and darkness appears not only in Seneca's poetry, but also in his prose. In the *Epistulae morales* he ridicules the bizarre lifestyle of his contemporaries, who sleep during the daytime and get up at night to enjoy themselves with wild feasts. He calls them *antipodes* — those who live upside down:

Sunt qui officia lucis noctisque perverterint nec ante diducant oculos hesterna graves
crapula quam adpetere nox coepit. Qualis illorum condicio dicitur, quos natura, ut ait

---

[196] The motif of light and darkness plays an important part in the sixth book of Virgil's *Eneid* (cf. F. Solmsen, *op. cit.*, p. 215), which, as we know, was a frequent source of literary inspiration for Seneca.

Vergilius, sedibus nostris subditos e contrario posuit, "nosque ubi primus equis Oriens adflavit anhelis, illis sera rubens accendit lumina Vesper" [Verg. Georg. 1, 250-251]: *talis horum contraria omnibus non regio, sed vita est. Sunt quidam in eadem urbe antipodes, qui, ut M. Cato ait, nec orientem umquam solem viderunt nec occidentem.* (*Epist.* 122, 2)

In the same letter he speaks of their bad consciences which make them hide in the darkness and avoid daylight:

Causa autem est ita vivendi quibusdam, non quia aliquid existiment noctem ipsam habere iucundius, sed quia nihil iuvat solitum, et gravis malae conscientiae lux est [...]. (*Epist.* 122, 14)

All the passages I have quoted as examples of the contrast technique have one feature in common: they are built on a clear antithesis, which is sometimes very marked,[197] as in *Thyestes*, or very sophisticated and quite allusive, as in the passage from *Hercules Oetaeus* quoted above.

The second kind of antithesis — the allusive — appears in the following passage of *Troades*, where Andromache says farewell to her son Astyanax just before his execution by Ulysses:

Fremitu leonis qualis audito tener
timidum iuvencus applicat matri latus,
at ille saevus matre summota leo
praedam minorem morsibus vastis premens
frangit vehitque: talis e nostro sinu
te rapiet hostis. [...]
(*Tro.* 794-799)

In this passage we can see a strong contrast between Ulysses and Astyanax. The former has been described as *saevus*, the latter as *tener*. There is therefore a contrast between strength and weakness, as well as between power and defencelessness. Seneca here uses the image of a lion, which was popular with ancient Greek poets.[198]

The comparison between Astyanax depicted as a weak calf and Ulysses depicted as a raging lion renders the contrast between the executioner-predator and the executed-prey as striking as possible. As in *Thyestes* and *Hercules Oetaeus*, here too

---

[197] Gustaw Przychocki treats these as stylistic figures (cf. *Styl tragedyj Anneusza Seneki*, Kraków 1946, pp. 43-44).

[198] Przychocki notes that most of Seneca's images are taken from nature and that they are meant to have an instant effect (cf. *ibidem*, p. 28). Some scholars interpret the animal similes as a direct allusion to the *venationes* and suggest that they *also encourage the audience to dehumanize Astyanax and consider him with the same regard as that given to animals killed for entertainment* [...]. (J. Shelton, *The spectacle of death in Seneca's "Troades"*, [in:] *Seneca in Performance*, p. 108).

70   Chapter III

the contrast between the positive element and the negative element implies the most basic contrast between good and evil.[199]

The final contrast, which is very typical of Seneca, is that between reason and madness, which is caused by an excess of passion. An excellent example is *Phaedra*, whose main character is driven to madness by her physical desire for her stepson Hippolytus.

In the following passage of the nurse's speech the contrast between sanity and madness is very marked:

Quotiens amabit Cressa? Ph. Quae memoras scio
vera esse, nutrix; sed furor cogit sequi
peiora.[200] *Vadit animus in praeceps sciens*
remeatque frustra sana consilia appetens.
(*Phae.* 177-180)

There is a very strong contrast between *sana consilia* and *furor*. The latter is, of course, the negative element of the pair. It becomes predominant and pushes Phaedra to obey her insane passion, totally eradicating the positive element, i.e. mental sobriety.

Another example of the use of the contrast between sanity and madness is that moment in *Hercules Furens* where the main character suddenly goes mad:

videat sub Ossa Pelion Chiron suum,
in caelum Olympus tertio positus gradu
perveniet aut mittetur. Am. Infandos procul
averte sensus; pectoris sani parum
magni tamen compesce dementem impetum.
(*HerF.* 971-975)

What is interesting is that Hercules' madness is juxtaposed with the sudden fall of night:

Venena cessent, nulla nocituro gravis
suco tumescat herba. Non saevi ac truces
regnent tyranni; si quod etiamnunc est scelus
latura tellus, properet, et si quod parat

---

[199] Even more fundamentally, such an essentialist reading of Thyestes (or indeed of any other Senecan play) is rooted in the attempt to preserve a diametrical opposition between "good" (perhaps even "Stoic") and "bad" characters, which in turn would ensure the viability of a didactic reading of the tragedies: the representation of unmitigated evil could then be seen to act as a deterrent. "Good" and "bad" qualities, of course, would also be bound to determine the public's reactions: approval and disgust, both ethical and aesthetic, would unify the moral and artistic dimensions of the plays. (A. Schiesaro, op. cit., p. 148).

[200] "Sequi peiora" recalls Ovid's neat encapsulation of the dilemma at Met. 7, 19-21. (Seneca, Phaedra, p. 108).

monstrum, meum sit. — Sed quid hoc? Medium diem
cinxere tenebrae. Phoebus obscuro meat
sine nube vultu. Quis diem retro fugat
agitque in ortus? Unde nox atrum caput
ignota profert? Unde tot stellae polum
implent diurnae? Primus en noster labor
caeli refulget parte non minima leo.
iraque totus fervet et morsus parat.
(*HerF.* 935-946)

Here, therefore, we have a very interesting fusion of two motifs: that of light and darkness is closely intertwined with that of sanity and madness. The hero's sanity, which is depicted as light, is suddenly conquered by *furor*, which is depicted as darkness — and, as happens in all Seneca's tragedies, the negative contrasting element overcomes the positive. This peculiar pessimism is quite typical of Seneca. The stronger the contrast, the greater the victory of evil. Beauty is defeated by ugliness, life by death, light by darkness and reason by madness.

To make things a little clearer, let us gather up all these motifs in the following simple table:

negative element (wins)	positive element (loses)
evil	good
ugliness	beauty
darkness	light
night	day
death	life
madness	reason

Scholars have long recognized that Seneca's style is anticlassical[201] and innovatory. We have also seen that he uses the contrast technique not only in poetry, but also in prose. The tragedies themselves are built on this contrast between an evil element (such as ugliness, darkness, death or madness) and a good element (such as beauty, light, life and reason). The struggle between the two opposing forces, however, is not an equal one. Evil always prevails over good and eventually destroys it.

This feature of the "represented world" of Seneca's tragedies greatly resembles the last two phases of Northrop Frye's theory of myths. Senecan tragedy unquestionably belongs to the sixth phase of tragedy (Frye himself attributes it to that phase[202]) — *a world of shock and horror in which the central images are images of spharagmos, that is, cannibalism, mutilation and torture.*[203]

---

[201] Cf. A. Traina, *op. cit.*, p. 10.
[202] *"Titus Andronicus" is an experiment in Senecan sixth-phase horror which makes a great deal of mutilation, and shows also a strong interest, from the opening scene on, in the sacrificial symbolism of tragedy.* (N. Frye, *Anatomy of Criticism...*, pp. 222-223).
[203] Cf. *ibidem*, p. 222.

In the final part of Seneca's *Thyestes* the chorus sings a song about the end of the world, the death of gods and humans and the return of chaos, which surprisingly matches Frye's description of the last phase of tragedy:[204]

Ipse insueto novus hospitio
Sol Auroram videt occiduus
tenebrasque iubet surgere nondum
nocte parata:
non succedunt astra nec ullo
micat igne polus,
non Luna gravis digerit umbras.
Sed quidquid id est, utinam nox sit!
Trepidant, trepidant pectora magno
percussa metu,
ne fatali cuncta ruina
quassata labent iterumque deos
hominesque premat deforme chaos,
iterum terras et mare cingens
et vaga picti sidera mundi
natura tegat.
(*Thy.* 822-834)

As in Frye's theory, the day (light) is the equivalent of order, while the night (darkness) is the equivalent of chaos.[205] The contrast technique is therefore also a means of defining the "represented world" as one which is on the brink of collapse. Night which dominates over light, ugliness which destroys beauty, or madness which eradicates reason are parts of a complex metaphor that depicts the great cataclysm to come.

As scholars have already discovered, the motif of the reversal of the sun had always been associated with the myth of the Pelopides and was used by Sophocles in his lost *Thyestes* as well as by Euripides in *Electra* (726 ff.), *Iphigenia Taurica*, (816) and *Orestes* (1001 ff.).[206] Seneca is therefore following a long dramatic tradition.[207]

Not everything in this passage has been taken from the Greeks, however.[208] Apart from the motif of the solar reversal, the whole passage can also be associated

---

[204] *The phases of tragedy move from the heroic to the ironic, the first three corresponding to the first three phases of romance, the last three to the last three of irony.* (*Ibidem*, p. 219).

[205] Cf. idem, *Collected Works on Renaissance Literature*, ed. by M. Dolzani, Toronto 2006, p. 17; cf. idem, *Fearful Symmetry*, Princeton 1969, p. 278.

[206] Cf. T. Rosenmeyer, *Senecan Drama*..., pp. 158-159.

[207] Cf. *ibidem*, pp. 158-159.

[208] As scholars have noted: *Interestingly enough, for all the emphasis that the reversal of the sun attracts in Thyestes, it lacks the prominence it had received in earlier texts, where it was credited with a fundamental cosmogonic function.* (A. Schiesaro, *op. cit.*, p. 95). *Ruin itself,*

with the Stoic concept of *finis mundi*. In his *Consolatio ad Marciam* Seneca depicts the end of the world (ἐκπύρωσις), which is to be reborn after the cataclysm:

Totos supprimet montes et alibi rupes in altum novas exprimet; maria sorbebit, flumina avertet et commercio gentium rupto societatem generis humani coetumque dissolvet; alibi hiatibus vastis subducet urbes, tremoribus quatiet et ex infimo pestilentiae halitus mittet et inundationibus quicquid habitatur obducet necabitque omne animal orbe submerso et ignibus vastis torrebit incendetque mortalia. Et cum tempus advenerit quo se mundus renovaturus extinguat, viribus ista se suis caedent et sidera sideribus incurrent et omni flagrante materia uno igni quicquid nunc ex disposito lucet ardebit. Nos quoque felices animae et aeterna sortitae, cum deo visum erit iterum ista moliri, labentibus cunctis et ipsae parva ruinae ingentis accessio in antiqua elementa vertemur. (Ad Mar. 26, 6-7).

In *Thyestes*, however, he ignores the optimistic ending of the Stoic myth and leaves us with the grim image of *Götterdämmerung*[209] and general destruction.

The motif of the victory of evil over good (represented by various metaphors) and the return of chaos would seem to be not only the fruit of Seneca's philosophical interests, but also some kind of *signum temporis* — an expression of the general atmosphere of fear and uncertainty in Nero's Rome. It was also a feature of the contemporary decadent taste of the time, which often delighted in cruelty and horror. In Nero's Rome there was hardly any place for mild aesthetic qualities[210] associated with beauty.[211] The qualities which were generally present in architecture and in popular culture[212] were strong qualities[213] associated with sublimity.[214]

Nero's reign was also a period of striking contrasts which permeated all spheres of human life. Life contrasted with death, danger with safety, beauty with ugliness, power with impotence and happiness with suffering. Seneca's literary technique can therefore also be considered to be a product of its time — so restless and so full of contrasts.

---

etymologically, is a "flowing", a rush and a collapse like that of overly wet clay. Cosmic flux is a favourite theme or image in the Stoic poets of the first century of our era. (T. Rosenmeyer, *Senecan Drama...*, p. 130).

[209] Cf. *ibidem*, p. 158.
[210] Cf. M. Wallis, *op. cit.*, pp. 198-199.
[211] Cf. E. Burke, *op. cit.*, p. 157.
[212] Cf. A. Futrell, *Blood in the Arena...*, pp. 48-49.
[213] Cf. M. Wallis, *op. cit*, p. 199.
[214] Cf. E. Burke, *op. cit.*, p. 157.

CHAPTER IV

The Aesthetics of Disgust

No passion so effectually robs the mind of all its powers of acting and reasoning as fear. For fear being an apprehension of pain or death, it operates in a manner that resembles actual pain. Whatever therefore is terrible, with regard to sight, is sublime too, whether this cause of terror be endued with greatness of dimensions or not; for it is impossible to look on anything as trifling, or contemptible, that may be dangerous.

Edmund Burke, *A Philosophical Enquiry into the Origin of our Ideas of the Sublime and Beautiful*[215]

In this chapter I would like to examine a matter which is essential for an understanding of the aesthetics of Senecan tragedy: the problem of ugliness and mutilation in these plays. This nightmarish world has been the subject of many discussions.[216]

Seneca's detailed descriptions of cruelty and the disfigurement of the human body obviously contrast with the principles of good taste set forward by Horace:

Segnius irritant animos demissa per aurem
quam quae sunt oculis subiecta fidelibus et quae
ipse sibi tradit spectator: non tamen intus
digna geri promes in scaenam multaque tolles
ex oculis, quae mox narret facundia praesens:
ne pueros coram populo Medea trucidet
aut humana palam coquat exta nefarius Atreus
aut in avem Procne vertatur, Cadmus in anguem.
(Hor. *Ars* 180-187)

---

[215] E. Burke, *op. cit.*, p. 101.
[216] Cf. O. Regenbogen, *op. cit.*, passim; cf. J. Smereka, *op. cit.*, pp. 615-650; cf. A. Schiesaro, *op. cit.*, passim; cf. J. Styka, *La littérature grecque à la lumière de l'appréciation esthétique des auteurs romains depuis Auguste jusqu'au IIe siècle après J.-Ch.*, transl. by B. Hrehorowicz, Wrocław 1987, p. 76; cf. R. Mayer, *op. cit.*, pp. 31-32.

In Seneca's tragedies Medea and Thyestes commit murders *coram populo*, which means "on stage". These plays, however, were more recited than acted out, so the cruel deeds were not seen by the audience (*oculis subiecta*), but heard (*demissa per aurem*) and imagined.

Horace believed that even the fullest verbal description was much less powerful than a living image. However, as Edmund Burke argues, a good poet or writer is able to give a far better idea of an object than even the greatest painter.[217]

Burke's theory is of great interest to anyone who wishes to examine the literary techniques of Seneca, for he was not only a philosopher and a poet, but also a real master of rhetoric.[218] He was also a great admirer of the two Augustan epic poets Virgil and Ovid, sharing a taste for rhetoric with the latter.

As we have seen in previous chapters, in Seneca's tragedies the narrative-descriptive element is often used as a substitute for direct presentation, as the plays were conceived as recitation tragedies and not as traditional stage tragedies.

The great power of words which is so characteristic of Seneca has already been recognized by scholars and also by other poets. As T.S. Eliot says in his famous essay: *in the plays of Seneca, the drama is all in the word.*[219]

If we take Burke's view that a good writer is able to paint a much better picture than the best of painters, we may begin to understand the power of Seneca's detailed descriptions, which in all probability were designed to excite the listener's (or reader's) imagination.

In the twentieth century another literary theorist, Wolfgang Iser — taking as his starting point Roman Ingarden's concept of "partially undetermined places" (*miejsca niedookreślenia*) in the structure of a work of literature[220] — elaborated the theory of so-called "blanks", which may be treated as complementary to the treatise of Burke.

Iser claims that literary texts, apart from their basic meaning, also contain some elements which themselves do not convey meaning and cannot be described but which can be "concretized" in the act of imagining. These are nothing more than little gaps in the description which can be filled in by the imagination of the reader. Iser calls them "blanks".[221]

---

[217] *On the other hand, the most lively and spirited verbal description I can give, raises a very obscure and imperfect idea of such objects; but then it is in my power to raise a stronger emotion by the description than I could do by the best painting.* (E. Burke, *op. cit.*, p. 4).

[218] Cf. J. Smereka, *op. cit.*, p. 615.

[219] Cf. T. S. Eliot, *op. cit.*, pp. 65-105; cf. D. Mastronarde, *op. cit.*, passim.

[220] Cf. R. Ingarden, *O dziele literackim*, Warszawa 1960, pp. 316-326 (§ 38 in chapter VII). Ingarden's book was originally published in German: idem, *Das literarische Kunstwerk*, Halle 1931; cf. idem, *The Literary Work of Art*, p. 246 (§ 38). Grabowicz's translation of Ingarden's term is "spots of indeterminacy of represented objectivities". The original German version is "Unbestimmtheitsstellen".

[221] *The text is a whole system of such processes, and so, clearly, there must be a place within this system for the person who is to perform the reconstituting. This place is marked by the gaps*

In the case of a precise description, the reader can "see" a fairly complete image of the object based on the details he already knows, but at the same time is given the freedom to fill in the gaps himself. The task of a good poet or writer is therefore to construct descriptions in such a way that the reader can "see" the most powerful images possible in his imagination.

In this context, Seneca's long and detailed descriptions of horrible, macabre and sometimes disgusting things appear to be very interesting. There are many such places in his tragedies. We will therefore now attempt to determine *how* and *why* he lays so much emphasis on death, disfigurement and ugliness. My own hypothesis is that he may have done so deliberately, perhaps in order to shock his audience or perhaps just to hold their attention.[222]

According to Seneca's philosophy, something can be ugly (*foedum; deforme*) both in a physical and in a moral sense. The exaggerated descriptions of *affectus* in his prose are the equivalent of the naturalistic descriptions of wounds and corpses in his poetry. The suffering of a mutilated soul is comparable to the suffering of a mutilated body, but people in general tend to fear the latter much more than the former.

Seneca knew this very well and in a few places in the *Epistulae morales* (82, 4; 123, 15; 124, 3) he mentions the fear of physical mutilation. In this light the highly visual character of Seneca's plays (especially in scenes where something terrifying happens or appears)[223] becomes somewhat easier to understand.

Although we also find shocking or extensive descriptions of death and mutilation in Seneca's philosophical works,[224] it is above all his prose that abounds in

---

in the text — it consists in the blanks which the reader is to fill in. They cannot, of course, be filled in by the system itself, and so it follows that they can only be filled in by another system. Whenever the reader bridges the gaps, communication begins. The gaps function as a kind of pivot on which the whole text-reader relationship revolves. Hence the structured blanks of the text stimulate the process of ideation to be performed by the reader on terms set by the text. (W. Iser, *The Act of Reading. A Theory of Aesthetic Response*, Baltimore 1981, p. 169).

[222] Cf. R. Mayer, *op. cit.*, pp. 31-32.

[223] *Seneca's tragedies are remarkable for their vivid, atmospheric descriptions of macabre and grotesque events. The strikingly visual character of his language, especially apparent in the depiction of gruesome occurrences, clearly separates Seneca as a tragedian from his fifth-century Greek predecessors, Aeschylus, Sophocles, and Euripides.* (E. R. Varner, *op. cit.*, p. 119). Cf. J. Smereka, *op. cit.*, passim.

[224] We do find descriptions of violent death in his prose, but Seneca does not dwell on them. Meltzer quotes one such passage: *Nam Telesphorum Rhodium amicum suum undique decurtatum, cum aures illi nasumque abscidisset, in cavea velut novum aliquod animal et inusitatum diu pavit, cum oris detruncati mutilatique deformitas humanam faciem perdidisset; accedebat fames et squalor et inluvies corporis in stercore suo destituti; callosis super haec genibus manibusque, quas in usum pedum angustiae loci cogebant, lateribus vero adtritu exulceratis non minus foeda quam terribilis erat forma eius visentibus, factusque poena sua monstrum misericordiam quoque amiserat. Tamen, cum dissimillimus esset homini qui illa patiebatur, dissimilior erat qui faciebat* (*De ira* 3, 17, 3-4). *The passage illustrates well an aim and method common to both the prose works and the tragedies of Seneca: the author asks us to consider the human soul's potential for*

colourful depictions of human passions. For example, at the beginning of *De ira* he gives a very vivid description of a man who is beside himself with rage.²²⁵ The man, however, is alive and the ugliness of his face, which is named *foeda visu* and *horrenda facies* is more ridiculous than terrible. This kind of ugliness is merely the result of a bad emotional state and not of physical mutilation. The caricature of the angry man is not meant to terrify the reader, but rather to make him realize just how miserable people who indulge their passions can appear to others.²²⁶

By contrast, the descriptions of physical mutilation in the tragedies seem to have quite a different purpose: in all probability they are meant to shock and terrify.²²⁷ They are also meant to hold the audience's attention, as they touch a deep human fear:

An. Quis Colchus hoc, quis sedis incertae Scytha
commissit, aut quae Caspium tangens mare
gens iuris ausa? Non Busiridis
puerilis aras sanguis aspersit feri,
nec parva gregibus membra Diomedis suis
epulanda posuit. Quis tuos artus teget
tumuloque tradet? Nun. Quos enim praeceps locus

---

evil, for the monstrous, by confronting us with shockingly brutal behavior. (G. Meltzer, *op. cit.*, p. 309). I argue that the aim of such passages in Seneca's prose is different from those in his poetry. In the former they serve only as occasional powerful examples of a heinous crime, whereas in the latter they are a means of conveying aesthetic pleasure.

²²⁵ *Nam ut furentium certa indicia sunt audax et minax vultus, tristis frons, torva facies, citatus gradus, inquietae manus, color versus, crebra et vehementius acta suspiria, ita irascentium eadem signa sunt: flagrant ac micant oculi, multus ore toto rubor exaestuante ab imis praecordiis sanguine, labra quatiuntur, dentes comprimuntur, horrent ac surriguntur capilli, spiritus coactus ac stridens, articulorum se ipsos torquentium sonus, gemitus mugitusque et parum explanatis vocibus sermo praeruptus et conplosae saepius manus et pulsata humus pedibus et totum concitum corpus "magnasque irae minas agens", foeda visu et horrenda facies depravantium se atque intumescentium — nescias utrum magis detestabile vitium sit an deforme.* (*De ira* 1, 1, 3-5).

²²⁶ According to Seneca, the physical appearance of a person mirrored his or her state of mind (cf. E. Wesołowska, *Postaci w "Medei" i "Fedrze" Seneki*, p. 37).

²²⁷ *Descriptions like this, of bloodthirsty violence and / or ghoulishness, play a prominent role in* Thyestes, *and are no isolated phenomenon there. In fact, a preoccupation with carnage and death may be said to be a characteristic of literature of the early Empire (or at least of certain authors of the period). Passages of this nature occur often in Seneca's plays and in Lucan, and more than occasionally in Statius'* Thebaid. *There is no real violence in what we have of Petronius'* Satyricon *but there certainly is morbidity and even ghoulishness, and ghoulishness, I think [...], is employed as a literary commonplace as early as the Augustan period, in the elegiac poetry of Tibullus and Propertius. In spite of its frequency of occurrence, this interest in carnage and death is a characteristic of Silver-Latin literature which has been ignored almost entirely by critics. When noticed, it is briefly and in pejorative terms. Those who do bother to give some explanation of the motif's inspiration usually attribute it to the effort to command the reader's shocked attention, or sometimes merely to a perverted Roman taste for blood.* (J. Park Poe, *op. cit.*, p. 356).

reliquit artus? Ossa disiecta et gravi
elisa casu; signa clari corporis,
et ora et illas nobiles patris notas,
confudit imam pondus ad terram datum;
soluta cervix silicis impulsu, caput
ruptum cerebro penitus expresso — iacet
deforme corpus. An. Sic quoque est similis patri.
(*Tro.* 1104-1117)

Scholars have already noted Seneca's fascination with the human body — both with its harmonious beauty and with its ugliness, disfigurement and decay.[228] A purely scientific fascination is one thing, however — individual taste is another. In Seneca's tragedies these two come together.

Another interesting thing about these plays is that descriptions of bodily mutilation often follow the personal defeat of one of the characters. The description of the self-blinding of Oedipus is a good illustration of this:

Scrutatur avidus manibus uncis lumina,
radice ab ima funditus vulsos simul
evolvit orbes; haeret in vacuo manus
et fixa penitus unguibus lacerat cavos
alte recessus luminum et inanes sinus
saevitque frustra plusque quam satis est furit.
Tantum est periclum lucis? Attollit caput
cavisque lustrans orbibus caeli plagas
noctem experitur. Quidquid effossis male
dependet oculis rumpit, et victor deos
conclamat omnis: "parcite en parcite, precor:
iam iusta feci, debitas poenas tuli;
inventa thalamis digna nox tandem meis."
Rigat ora foedus imber et lacerum caput
largum revulsis sanguinem venis vomit.
(*Oed.* 965-979).

The messenger speech ends abruptly at this point. This suddenness is probably no coincidence, especially as the description is particularly gruesome.[229] As the

---

[228] *Something other than fear of death, or weariness with suffering, inspires the gusto with which here Seneca describes the cutting up and cooking of dead bodies. This is more than merely negative. That is, more is involved than the poet's horrified revulsion from the circumstances of his environment. An intellectual synthesis has taken place (whatever the elements of the synthesis may be), for the poet is not simply recoiling from horror in a normal and predictable way. Of course this fascination with death — particularly the grisly physical details of death — is a perverted thing. The poet invites his readers to participate vicariously in an experience which is both sadistic and masochistic.* (Ibidem, p. 358). Cf. A. J. Boyle, *Tragic Seneca...*, p. 134.

[229] *[...] although Sophocles is unwontedly descriptive in his account of Oedipus' blinding (O. T. 1276ff.), Seneca enlarges on this moment with a characteristic taste for the grotesque*

macabre vision is the last element of the speech, it is the first one to be "seen" by the reader (or rather the listener) with his "mind's eye".

It would therefore seem that Seneca expressly designed his descriptions to make his audience vividly imagine a shocking spectacle. A characteristic feature of his tragedies is his highly visual style. Moreover, he often peppers the text with "stage directions". These, however, are not for the use of actors, but are designed to guide the audience towards a "proper" filling in of "blanks" in the text of the play.[230] In other words, the listener or reader is told what he must "see" in his imagination.

A good example of this strategy is that passage of *Phaedra* where Theseus sees the mangled body of Hippolytus being brought in by servants:

Th. Huc, huc, reliquias vehite cari corporis
pondusque et artus temere congestos date.
Hippolytus hic est? [...]
[...]
Complectere artus, quodque de nato est super,
miserande, maesto pectore incumbens, fove.
Disiecta, genitor, membra laceri corporis
in ordinem dispone et errantes loco
restitue partes: fortis hic dextrae locus,
hic laeva frenis docta moderandis manus
ponenda: laevi lateris agnosco notas.
Quam magna lacrimis pars adhuc nostris abest!
(*Phae.* 1247-1249; 1254-1261)

In this scene Seneca probably imitates the lost final scene of the *Bacchae* of Euripides,[231] but with a different purpose.[232] According to one hypothesis, Seneca lacked a sense of humour and failed to realize that naturalism such as this could be ridiculous.[233] On the other hand, it is hardly likely that such an expert on rhetoric as Seneca was would not know what effect his writing might have on an audience. The

---

(*Oed.* 958-979) *which outdoes the Sophoclean description in length and vividness.* (V. Tietze Larson, *op. cit.*, p. 39). What Tietze Larson here terms "grotesque" would, in my opinion, be better described as "sheer horror".

[230] Cf. W. Iser, *op. cit.*, p. 169.
[231] Cf. R. Mayer, *op. cit.*, p. 32.
[232] *What was probably very moving in Euripides is generally deemed laughable in Seneca. But if, as was urged above, the final scene is meant not to be seen but imagined, then much of the objection evaporates.* (*Ibidem*, p. 32).
[233] *The command to reassemble Hippolytus has been condemned for poor taste* [...]. *There is, however, a confusion here between fact and fantasy. It may indeed have been a moral duty in antiquity to reassemble a broken corpse, but how such a scene is described depends on the writer. S. lacked a sense of humour and he failed to perceive that an over-explicit description becomes funny or wearisome.* (Seneca, *Phaedra*, p. 195).

only conclusion, therefore, must be that his purpose was to shock and terrify, thus overstepping all the boundaries of classical "good taste".[234]

A possible confirmation of this are the "stage directions" in line 1247, where Theseus orders the servants to lay down his dead son. The words are in fact not addressed to the actors, but to the listener's imagination. Seneca guides his listeners and readers so that they can fill in the "blanks" in the text just as he wishes.[235]

Seneca would seem to have had a visual kind of imagination. His plays contain many reminiscences of what he may have seen or what may have been described to him. Many of his "stage directions" — apart from being conventional (or, perhaps, serving the purposes of public recitation) — are totally inconsistent and are therefore of no use to a stage director.[236]

Like his Greek predecessors, Seneca uses messengers[237] to relate events that he cannot or does not wish to show directly "on stage". Normally it is the messenger who relates the καταστροφή. For example, in *Phaedra* Seneca follows the Euripidean manner of relating the death of Hippolytus:[238]

Euripides:
αὐτὸς δ' ὁ τλήμων ἡνίαισιν ἐμπλακεὶς
δεσμὸν δυσεξήνυστον ἕλκεται δεθείς,
σποδούμενος μὲν πρὸς πέτραις φίλον κάρα
θραύων τε σάρκας, δεινὰ δ' ἐξαυδῶν κλύειν·
Στῆτ', ὦ φάνταισι ταῖς ἐμαῖς τεθραμμέναι,
μή μ' ἐξαλείψητ' ὦ πατρὸς τάλαιν' ἀρά.
(Eur. *Hipp.* 1236-1241)

Seneca:
Late cruentat arva et inlisum caput
scopulis resultat; auferunt dumi comas,
et ora durus pulcra populatur lapis
peritque multo vulnere infelix decor.[239]
(*Phae.* 1093-1096)

---

[234] On Seneca's "gothic" taste see: J. Pypłacz, *"Gotyckie" elementy w tragediach Seneki*, "Symbolae Philologorum Posnaniensium Graecae et Latinae" 2008, XVIII, p. 284.

[235] *Description in Senecan tragedy [...] operates entirely in the narrative mode. That is to say, it is not there to facilitate the presentation of the action to the audience through spectacle for the immediate apprehension of their own senses; rather it is part of the author's indirect presentation of the action to the imaginative faculty of the audience, as he acts as the audience's eyes and ears.* (V. Tietze Larson, *op. cit.*, pp. 55-56).

[236] Cf. Seneca, *Troades...*, p. 39.

[237] Cf. T. Wikarjakówna, *Rola zwiastuna w tragedii greckiej*, "Symbolae Philologorum Posnaniensium" 1979, IV, p. 5.

[238] Cf. Ch. Segal, *Senecan Baroque. The Death of Hippolytus in Seneca, Ovid, and Euripides*, "Transactions of the American Philological Association" 1984, 114, p. 323.

[239] The expression: *et ora durus pulcra populatur lapis* is almost a Latin translation of: σποδούμενος μὲν πρὸς πέτραις φίλον κάρα.

As scholars have pointed out, Seneca's description has to some extent also been influenced by Ovid's version of this scene:[240]

Excutior curru, lorisque tenentibus artus
viscera viva trahi, nervos in stipe teneri,
membra rapi partim, partim reprensa relinqui,
ossa gravem dare fracta sonum fessamque videres
exhalari animam nullasque in corpore partes,
noscere quas posses, unumque erat omnia vulnus.
(Ovid. *Met.* 15, 524-529)

This time, however, Seneca is competing not with Ovid, but with Euripides himself. His own description is much more gruesome, as he does not shrink from showing all the dreadful details.[241] For Euripides, the death of Hippolytus was mainly a source of ἔλεος, as the messenger laments the death of his beloved master. Seneca for his part lays more emphasis on the destruction of Hippolytus' beauty: his messenger speaks of *ora pulcra*, i.e. the beautiful face, mutilated by the rough stone. It is not the loss of the young man's life, but the loss of his beauty — *infelix decor*[242] — that is the subject of the messenger's sorrow.

This leads us to another of Seneca's favourite techniques — that of "tragic revelation".[243] At the end of *Thyestes* he displays the amputated heads and hands of the sons of the principal character:

Abscisa cerno capita et avulsas manus
et rupta fractis cruribus vestigia —
hoc est quod avidus capere non potuit pater.
(*Thy.* 1038-1044)

The climax of the play is very strong,[244] as it comes all of a sudden and the terrible details are revealed all at once.

Although Seneca did not shrink from showing the most terrible and macabre scenes, such as murders, suicides and decaying corpses, he did often choose to leave certain events "off stage" — not out of deference to classical principles, but merely for the sake of the integrity of the plot. Most probably he concentrated only on the most powerful images and those which, taken together, would make the greatest

---

[240] Cf. Ch. Segal, *Senecan Baroque...*, p. 323.

[241] Cf. Seneca, *Phaedra*, p. 183; cf. J. Smereka, *op. cit.*, p. 639.

[242] *It was the beauty of Hippolytus which attracted Phaedra, so the course operates against it chiefly.* (Seneca, *Phaedra*, p. 183). This was a perfect opportunity for Seneca to highlight the unequal contest between beauty and ugliness, which was one of his favourite themes.

[243] Cf. A. J. Boyle, *The Canonic Text: Virgil's Aeneid*, [in:] *Roman Epic*, ed. by idem, London 1993, p. 90.

[244] *abscisa ... avulsas ... rupta fractis: the appalling climax of the play's many instances of "breaking" and "sundering" language.* (Seneca, *Thyestes*, p. 234).

possible impression. Events which were less powerful were simply relegated to "off stage" status or merely mentioned in passing.

In *Medea*, for example, he condenses the messenger's account of the death of Creusa and her father to two lines, whereas Euripides gives a detailed description of their horrible death (1167-1230). It would seem that in this instance Seneca did not care to emulate Euripides' brutal naturalism, as there was little here that he could have done better. He therefore contents himself with the following lines:

Periere cuncta, concidit regni status;
nata atque genitor cinere permixto iacent.
(*Med.* 879-880)

There is one other possible reason for such a condensation: Seneca did not want to delay the scene in which Medea murders her sons[245] and which he intended to display directly in all its horror. The difference between the two authors is that whereas Euripides contents himself with frightening the audience, Seneca does his utmost to reduce it to a state of shock.

Having two ghastly murders in two parts of the play might also have weakened the final scene, by which Seneca had set such great store. This he avoided by reducing the account of Creusa's death to the absolute minimum.

Instead of repeating the Euripidean scheme,[246] he aimed to move his audience in another way — by making them witness a terrible murder. Medea therefore slays her own sons *coram populo*. Seneca achieves the powerful effect of ἐνάργεια by means of concurrent narration, meaning that an event is related by one (or more) of the characters at the same time as it is happening.

In *Troades* we can observe a similar strategy. In the centre of the "represented world" we have the messenger speech about the death of Astyanax and Polyxena. In order to emphasize it, Seneca had to diminish the account of Priam's execution.

An excellent example of this technique of "reducing" certain events in order to emphasize others is *Hercules Furens*. In this tragedy Hercules strikes twice: he kills the usurper Lycus and then, as a result of Juno's anger, he goes mad and murders his own family. In order to highlight the murder of Megara and her sons, which he has chosen to show *coram populo*, Seneca reduces the account of the killing of Lycus by including it in Hercules' monologue, which takes on the function of a messenger's speech.

---

[245] *It is characteristic of Greek tragedy that a messenger should arrive at a climactic point and deliver a long and elaborate account of some event vital to the plot which has happened off-stage. Sen. too uses this technique elsewhere, e. g. Phae 1000-1114, where a messenger reports at great length the appalling fate of Hippolytus; but in our play he is terse and gives only a bald outline of the disaster. [...] The reason seems to be that Sen. does not wish to halt the gathering momentum of the play, now moving towards the greater climax of the killing of the children which marks M.'s completed revenge.* (Seneca, Medea, p. 150).

[246] Ovid and the republican tragedians had already emulated it so many times that there may have been nothing left for Seneca to do if he wished above all to be original.

By contrast, he presents the death of Megara directly, together with a running commentary by Amphitryon, who witnesses the event:[247]

In coniugem nunc clava libratur gravis:
perfregit ossa, corpori trunco caput
abest nec usquam est. [...]
(*HerF.* 1024-1026)

The witness gives us a naturalistic description of the cruel murder: Megara is horribly mutilated and, like Hippolytus in *Phaedra*, is transformed in one moment into a disfigured corpse. Thanks to Amphitryon's commentary, the listener also becomes an eyewitness to the scene in his imagination.

As far as simultaneous commentaries are concerned, in *Agamemnon* there is a very original solution for the καταστροφή. We learn about the murder of Agamemnon from Cassandra, who — being endowed with the power to see things which she does not physically witness — informs us about the killing as it takes place, giving us this very detailed description of the murder scene:

Habet. Peractum est. Pendet exigua male
caput amputatum parte et hinc trunco cruor
exundat, illinc ora cum fremitu iacent.
Nondum recedunt: ille iam exanimem petit
laceratque corpus, illa fodientem adiuvat.
Uterque tanto scelere respondet suis:
est hic Thyestae natus, haec Helenae soror.
(*Ag.* 901-907)

She speaks of the badly amputated head and other disgusting details with an *insolita molestaque perspicuitas*,[248] so that the listener can easily witness the immense horror of the scene in his imagination.[249] The knowledge that Cassandra can clearly see everything thanks to her prophetic powers fully compensates the audience for

---

[247] Cf. J. Smereka, *op. cit.*, p. 634 ff.

[248] *Mortes et caedes de quibus nuntius legentes certiores facit, hoc proprium habent, quod insolitam molestamque perspicuitatem spirant. Agamemnonis caedes quae a Cassandra narratur, brevissime adumbrari videtur* [...]. (*Ibidem*, p. 636). Littlewood interprets this part of Cassandra's description as being full of malicious joy: *Cassandra is consumed by the desire for revenge and her metamorphosis from the unwilling seer of 720 ff. to the malicious viewer who delivers the second description of Agamemnon's murder (867-909) is achieved through her deviation from the model offered by Aeneas' response to Deiphobus and his Trojan ghosts.* (*op. cit.*, p. 219). *Seneca does little in this passage to justify his reputation for indiscriminate gore. The physical precision of the brief description is matched on the stylistic level by an approximation of a golden line (exigua male caput amputatum parte = a b C B A, cf. Canter 175).* (Seneca, *Agamemnon*, p. 343).

[249] *Atque quo plenius* διατύπωσις *reddatur, poeta de aspectu, quem occisus vir praestat, disserit (v. 901 sqq.).* (J. Smereka, *op. cit.*, p. 636).

the fact that the murder takes place within the palace and is not presented *coram populo*.

We have a similar situation in *Thyestes*, where the murder scene is not presented directly but is related in profuse detail by a messenger, who gives a very graphic description of the corpses:

> Nun. **Stetit** *sui securus et non est preces*
> *perire frustra passus; ast illi ferus*
> *in vulnere ensem abscondit et penitus premens*
> *iugulo manum commisit: educto* **stetit**
> *ferro cadaver, cumque dubitasset diu*
> *hac parte an illa caderet, in patruum cadit.*
> *Tunc ille ad aras Plisthenem saevus trahit*
> *adicitque fratri; colla percussa amputat;*
> *cervice caesa truncus in pronum ruit,*
> *querulum cucurrit murmure incerto caput.*
> (*Thy.* 720-729)

Each of the sons of Thyestes dies in a different way, but the descriptions of their deaths have one thing in common: they are macabre in their naturalism. For example, in the passage quoted above Seneca describes a headless corpse which for a while does not fall down but remains standing, like a living person,[250] while the head rolls on the ground muttering unintelligibly.[251] Seneca doubles the effect by repeating the form *stetit* twice: the first time he uses it to refer to the living Tantalus (*stetit sui securus*, 720), while three lines later he uses it to refer to his headless corpse.[252]

---

[250] Tarrant points out Seneca's emphasis on the state of physical death: Cadaver*: pointedly emphatic: what remained erect was a mere corpse. In general* cadaver *is a more highly charged word than* corpus, *carrying a stronger sense of the physical realities of death* [...]. (Seneca, Thyestes, p. 194).

[251] On the Ovidian inspiration for this passage see: *ibidem*, p. 195. *Atreus' uncertainty about whom first to kill is paralleled by the corpse's long hesitation about where to fall. After standing for "a long time" (*diu*) in deliberation, the corpse finally decides to fall on Atreus (723-25). The black humor of the incident comes from the incongruity of the corpse's deliberation and protest.* [...] *But the joke is also on Atreus, whose meticulous preparations cannot prevent the indignity of having a corpse fall on him. The black comedy continues as Plisthenes' corpse also makes a final, feeble gesture of protest: his truncated head rolls off his body murmuring incoherently (728-29). The chaotic slaughter contrasts with the ritual precision with which Atreus dissects the bodies and inspects the entrails (755-63).* (G. Meltzer, *op. cit.*, p. 325).

[252] Lucan imitated this passage: [...] *conpressum turba stetit omne cadaver* (Luc. *Phars.* 4, 787). Charles Martindale analyses Lucan's "wit" in this passage: *The climatic word* cadaver *is connected etymologically with* cadere, *"to fall", so that the abnormal situation is piquantly described in terms of something that stands falling.* (*Latin Poetry and the Judgement of Taste. An Essay in Aesthetics*, Oxford — New York 2005, p. 229). It is, however, Seneca's "wit" that Lucan is imitating.

Hearing all this, the members of the chorus enjoin the messenger to tell them about Atreus' crime (*effare, et istud pande, quodcumque est, malum*, 633) and — as it is revealed — they impatiently demand yet more appalling details:[253]

Nun. Exhorruistis? Hactenus si stat nefas,
pius est. Cho. An ultra maius aut atrocius
natura recipit? Nun. Sceleris hunc finem putas?
Gradus est. Cho. Quid ultra potuit? Obiecit feris
lanianda forsan corpora atque igne arcuit?
(*Thy.* 744-748)

Not content with this, they even suggest that Atreus may have committed some other atrocities and ask the messenger if, by any chance, he had not thrown the corpses to wild beasts (*obiecit feris lanianda*). This is probably an allusion to the *damnatio ad bestias*[254] which was so popular in Nero's Rome.

In order to satisfy their perverse curiosity, the messenger gives a full account of all the most revolting details of the crime:

Postquam hostiae placuere, securus vacat
iam fratris epulis: ipse divisum secat
in membra corpus, amputat trunco tenus
umeros patentis et lacertorum moras,
denudat artus durus atque ossa amputat;
tantum ora servat et datas fidei manus.
Haec veribus haerent viscera et lentis data
stillant caminis, illa flammatus latex
candente aeno iactat. Impositas dapes
transiluit ignis inque trepidantes focos
bis ter regestus et pati iussus moram
invitus ardet. Stridet in veribus iecur;
nec facile dicas corpora an flammae gemant:
gemuere. Piceos ignis in fumos abit;
et ipse fumus, tristis ac nebula gravis
non rectus exit seque in excelsum levat:
ipsos penates nube deformi obsidet.
(*Thy.* 759-775)

When he has finished recounting the murder and the preparations for the feast, he depicts the moment when Thyestes — who is ignorant of what

---

[253] *Throughout the messenger's account of the sacrifice, Atreus' lust for revenge, described in epic similes comparing him to a lion or tiger (707-13, 732-41), contrasts strongly with the cold precision of the slaughter, which is described in graphic, anatomical detail (760-63).* (G. Meltzer, *op. cit.*, p. 325).

[254] Cf. Seneca, *Thyestes*, p. 197.

has happened and is already half drunk — devours the bodies of his own sons:[255]

O Phoebe patiens, fugeris retro licet
medioque ruptum merseris caelo diem,
sero occidisti — lancinat gnatos pater
artusque mandit ore funesto suos;
Nitet fluente madidus unguento comam
gravisque vino; saepe praeclusae cibum
tenuere fauces — in malis unum hoc tuis
bonum est, Thyesta, quod mala ignoras tua.
(*Thy.* 776-783)

The description of Thyestes dining is remarkable for its extremely precise and graphic character. Particularly striking are the negative meanings of the words which refer to the action of eating.[256] Here we can notice a gradation: first Seneca uses the verb *mandit*, which is relatively neutral, but he adds the expression *ore funesto*, which is very strong. The expression *tenuere fauces* depicts Thyestes' beastly voracity.

This and other similar passages should be interpreted in a wider, historical and cultural context. Seneca's times were times of cruel spectacles and perverse customs, one of which was Caligula's idea of feeding the wild animals used in the games with prisoners[257] instead of sheep.

Thyestes is undoubtedly the boldest and cruellest of all the tragedies of Seneca.[258] It is the cruellest not only because of its shocking plot, but also because of its composition and the fact that in the centre of its "represented world" Seneca places an appalling crime, whose description is very long and detailed.

The atrocities unfold gradually. They begin with the entrance of the messenger, who starts his narrative with the description of a *locus terribilis* (623 ff.) and proceeds to give an account of the murder of the sons of Thyestes and the preparation

---

[255] Thyestes himself is presented as a repulsive character: *As for Thyestes, Seneca takes some care to convey to the audience an impression of Thyestes' uncleanness, emphasizing the repulsiveness of his appearance as he eats his meal and afterwards. He is a greasy, disgusting creature, head glistening with oil and heavy with wine (780-81, 948, 909-11).* (J. Park Poe, *op. cit.*, p. 369).

[256] Lancinat: *the shockingly violent word is placed first, its effect heightened still further by the long build-up in 776-78. Thyestes "rending" and "chewing" (mandit) contrast sharply with the antiseptic neatness of Atreus' preparation [...]; he seems to be amply fulfilling Atreus' vision,* liberos avidus pater / gaudensque laceret *(277-78).* (Seneca, *Thyestes*, p. 202).

[257] [...] *ad saginam ferarum muneri praeparatarum carius pecudes compararentur, ex noxiis laniandos adnotavit.* (Suet. Calig. 27, 1). Cf. D. Kyle, *op. cit.*, p. 186.

[258] *Longissima (v. 625-778) caedis atrocissimarumque rerum explicatio, ubi Seneca ἐξ ὄψεως summam et culmen adeptus est, in fabula quae "Thyestes" inscribitur, obviam nobis venit.* (J. Smereka, *op. cit.*, p. 641).

of a meal made from their bodies. He then describes the supper and conveys a terrifying image of Thyestes eating the flesh of his own children. At the end of the story we have a *tragic revelation*: Atreus shows Thyestes the heads and hands of his sons (1005 ff.).[259] Between this last scene and the end of the supper, however, there is a long passage of suspense, when the audience already know what has happened but Thyestes does not:

Th. Satias dapis me nec minus Bacchi tenet.
Augere cumulus hic voluptatem potest,
si cum meis gaudere felici datur.
(*Thy.* 973-975)

Assuming his brother's ignorance, Atreus begins a session of sophisticated mental torture.[260] He suggests to the happy and half-drunk man that he is already with his sons:[261]

At. Hic esse natos crede in amplexu patris.
Hic sunt eruntque; nulla pars prolis tuae
tibi subtrahetur. Ora quae exoptas dabo
totumque turba iam sua implebo patrem.
(*Thy.* 976-979)

---

[259] Cf. Seneca, *Thyestes*, p. 230.

[260] *Through his clever, sadistic jokes, Atreus seeks to ridicule his victim's dreadful predicament. Indeed, Atreus successfully uses Thyestes himself as his instrument of revenge, playing on his brother's moral weaknesses.* (G. Meltzer, *op. cit.*, p. 329).

[261] *Prolonging the pleasure of his revelation* [...], *Atreus indulges in a series of ghastly double entendres (a more elaborate version of the taunt used by Ovid's Procne at a similar moment, "intus habes quem poscis.", Met. 6. 655).* (Seneca, *Thyestes*, p. 226). Meltzer notes that Atreus' entire speech is filled with puns and black humor: *Throughout this speech, which is filled with black humor, Atreus uses puns and double entendres to play on the dismemberment and ingestion of Thyestes' children. For example, he assures Thyestes that "no part" of his children will be taken away from him and that he will be filled with their presence (977-79). Atreus puns on* ora *when he tells his brother that he will soon see the "faces" of his children; he applies a variation on the joke when, showing Thyestes the severed heads of his children, he asks if he recognizes them. Atreus, in assuring Thyestes that his need to see his children will be "satisfied"* (satiaberis, ne metue [980]), *cruelly plays on the physical satisfaction Thyestes expressed in the meal* (satias dapis [973]). *Atreus' mock reassurance implies, as well, that the banquet is fitting punishment for Thyestes' appetite for power. But Atreus' pun on Thyestes' "satisfaction" also calls to mind the tyrant's own obsessive need to satisfy his revenge. In his supposed concern for his guest's complete satisfaction and comfort, Atreus continues his grotesque parody of the genteel host.* [...] *Atreus' use of the subject matter, mood, and style of comedy heightens the horror of the banquet. His grotesque parody of a comic feast is ghastly, to be sure, yet strangely appropriate in a play obsessed with the theme of eating. Indeed, unrestrained, perverse appetites, both literal and figurative, are the subject of the play.* (*op. cit.*, p. 316).

Despite the strange physical symptoms he experiences (985 ff), Thyestes still remains unaware of what has happened to his sons (*natisque parcat*, 996; *redde iam gnatos mihi!*, 997).

Between the end of the banquet and the terrible ἀναγνώρισις there are twenty-nine lines of suspense. Thyestes waits impatiently for the truth to be made known, while the audience wait to witness the final interaction between the two brothers.

To recapitulate, in the composition of his plays Seneca applies the following strategies:

1. He builds up dramatic tension by means of a gradation of horrors[262] (the messenger reveals the dreadful events step by step, from the less expressive to the most expressive). This gradation ends with a tragic revelation of something utterly appalling (such as the heads of the sons of Thyestes or the disfigured body of Hippolytus in *Phaedra*).
2. He depicts all the macabre details in a very naturalistic way, so that the listener can "see" them in his imagination (as in *Troades*, *Hercules Furens*, *Phaedra* and *Thyestes*).
3. He minimizes some events in order to accentuate others (as with the death of Creusa in *Medea*).
4. The scenes of καταστροφή are concurrently related by one of the characters (as in *Hercules Furens*, where Amphitryon recounts the murder of Megara).
5. He also emphasizes the transformation of something which is aesthetically pleasant, e.g. a handsome youth, into something which is aesthetically repulsive, e.g. a mutilated corpse (as in *Phaedra*[263]).

Ugly things have been portrayed by artists since the most ancient times and we can find depictions of physical ugliness among the most famous works of Greek and Roman art.[264] Ugliness, however, was here kept at a certain distance.

In Greece the poet who discovered the aesthetic power of ugliness was Euripides, while in Rome it was Ovid, who in the *Metamorphoses* was the first Roman poet to make such use of "sharp" (i.e. negative) aesthetic qualities connected with ugliness, using them as a means of artistic expression. The sixth book contains quite brutal and naturalistic descriptions of physical suffering and mutilation in the stories of Tereus (412-674) and Marsyas (382-400).[265]

In the works of these writers, however, ugliness is almost always dominated by beauty and remains in classical harmony with the prevalent, mild aesthetic qualities.

---

[262] *In scaenis crudelissima facinora continentibus, tria coloris nostri instrumenta*, διατύπωσιν *dico eamque saepius sufflatam et molestam, gradationem et retardationem praeter verborum figurarumque ornatum primas acturas esse partes iam hic praemonendum est.* (J. Smereka, op. cit., p. 634).

[263] Cf. *ibidem*, p. 639.

[264] Cf. U. Eco, *Historia brzydoty*, p. 19.

[265] Some scholars suggest that Ovid's choice of subject may have been inherited from Hellenistic and neoteric poetry (cf. B. Otis, *Ovid As an Epic Poet*, Cambridge 1966, p. 206).

There were some things, therefore, which even Euripides and Ovid did not dare to show. By contrast, Seneca was the first poet who not only used ugliness, but exploited it to the full as a powerful means of expression. In his works ugliness is both aggressive and overwhelming and stands in the centre of the "represented world". Its main manifestation is the violent mutilation of a human body. In Senecan plays the mere death of a character is not enough. He or she has to die in the most appalling way.

Seneca may have been somewhat obsessed with death,[266] but this alone cannot account for his insistence on highlighting the gruesome details of extremely violent deaths in his tragedies. Most probably he was aware of his audience's appetite for negative aesthetic qualities[267] and catered for them accordingly,[268] He knew and perhaps subconsciously shared their fascination with cruel spectacles, which he officially disdained, but which he occasionally alluded to in his plays.[269] This fascination is particularly evident in his tragedies of *gloom, horror and abnormality*.[270]

We must remember that Roman taste was different from that of the Greeks. The favourite festive pastime of the Athenians was the theatre, but for the Romans — especially during Nero's reign — it was the amphitheatre, where performers actually died during each spectacle.

The amphitheatre,[271] along with the general political atmosphere during the early Empire,[272] had its part in the shaping of contemporary Roman taste. Seneca wrote his tragedies in a particular cultural and historical context and they are evidence of the taste of his day.[273] Not only do they mirror the taste of the early empire, they also portray the mentality of many of its citizens:

nunc saeva cautes, undique adfusa ducum
plebisque turba cingitur, totum coit
ratibus relictis vulgus. [...]
(*Tro.* 1076-1078)

---

[266] Cf. G. Jantzen, *Death and the Displacement of Beauty*, London 2004, p. 316; cf. J. Shelton, *op. cit.*, p. 87.

[267] Cf. E. R. Varner, *op. cit.*, p. 119.

[268] *In the field of aesthetic stimuli, signs are bound by a necessity that is rooted in the perceptual habits of the addressee (otherwise known as his taste): rhyme, meter, a more or less conventional sense of proportion, the need for verisimilitude, other stylistic concerns.* (U. Eco, *The Open Work*, p. 36).

[269] Cf. R. Mayer, *op. cit.*, p. 32; cf. M. Leigh, *op. cit.*, pp. 263, 281; cf. J. Shelton, *op. cit.*, passim.

[270] Cf. D. Mastronarde, *op. cit.*, p. 301.

[271] Cf. R. Mayer, *op. cit.*, p. 32.

[272] Cf. Ch. Segal, *Senecan Baroque...*, p. 313.

[273] Cf. W. H. Friedrich, *Die Raserei des "Hercules"* (1967), [in:] *Senecas Tragödien*, p. 142 ff.

In actual fact the Greek spectators are not Greek at all. Their avid curiosity and *Blutdurst* is purely Roman and the scene — the public execution of Astyanax — is nothing less than the execution of a prisoner, such as was practised in Roman amphitheatres during the games.[274]

As a poet, the son of a teacher of rhetoric and an aspiring successor to Virgil and Ovid, Seneca knew only too well what the power of a good description was. His aim was to move and even to shock[275] his audience. This was no easy task, as contemporary taste was strongly influenced by the cruelty of the amphitheatre.[276] Looking for new ways of making an impression on his audience, Seneca came up with the artistic depiction of extreme physical suffering and destruction. In creating images of horror, he was not averse to recounting the most disgusting and disturbing details in order to enable his listeners to see them in their imaginations. We may call this feature of Senecan tragedy his aesthetic of disgust.

---

[274] Cf. D. Kyle, *op. cit.*, p. 91.

[275] Along with the contemporary aesthetics of ἔκπληξις: Ὄγκου καὶ μεγαληγορίας καὶ ἀγῶνος ἐπὶ τούτους, ὦ νεανία, καὶ αἱ φαντασίαι παρασκευαστικώταται· οὕτω γοῦν <ἡμεῖς>, εἰδωλοποιίας <δ'> αὐτὰς ἔνιοι λέγουσι· καλεῖται μὲν γὰρ κοινῶς φαντασία πᾶν τὸ ὁπωσοῦν ἐννόημα γεννητικὸν λόγου παριστάμενον· ἤδη δ' ἐπὶ τούτων κεκράτηκε ὅταν ἃ λέγεις ὑπ' ἐνθουσιασμοῦ καὶ πάθους βλέπειν δοκῇς καὶ ὑπ' ὄψιν τιθῇς τοῖς ἀκούουσιν. ὡς δ' ἕτερόν τι ἡ ῥητορικὴ φαντασία βούλεται καί ἕτερον ἡ παρὰ ποιηταῖς οὐκ ἂν λάθοι σε, οὐδ' ὅτι τῆς μὲν ἐν ποιήσει τέλος ἐστὶν ἔκπληξις, τῆς δ' ἐν λόγοις ἐνάργεια, ἀμφότεραι δ' ὅμως τό τε <παθητικὸν> ἐπιζητοῦνται καὶ τὸ συγκεκινημένον. (Pseud. Long. 15, 1); *ἔκπληξις is surprise or fear which "knocks you out"; less often (e.g. Pl. Protag.) it is used of other violent feelings. From an early date it is associated with the effect of the startling and fantastic* [...]. (Pseudo-Longinus, *On the Sublime*, ed. with an introd. and comm. by D. A. Russell, Oxford 1964, p. 122). *The rhetorical figure of* enargeia, *the vivid image "painted" in words (*evidentia, sub oculos subiectio*), is here translated into creation of a shared subjective experience.* (R. Macksey, *Longinus Reconsidered*, "Modern Language Notes" 1993, 108, 5, Comparative Literature, p. 920).

[276] Cf. R. Mayer, *op. cit.*, pp. 31-32.

CHAPTER V

Musa Crudelis
The Birth of a New Aesthetic

> *This deep world*
> *Of darkness do we dread?*
>
> John Milton, *Paradise Lost*[277]

> [...] *beauty should be smooth, and polished; the great, rugged and negligent; beauty should shun the right line, yet deviate from it insensibly; the great in many cases loves the right line, and when it deviates, it often makes a strong deviation; beauty should not be obscure; the great ought to be dark and gloomy; beauty should be light and delicate; the great ought to be solid, and even massive.*
>
> Edmund Burke, *A Philosophical Enquiry into the Origin of our Ideas of the Sublime and Beautiful*[278]

In the previous chapters I have discussed the most significant features of Senecan tragedy, such as their affinity with epic poetry (ch. I), their style (ch. II), the presence of the macabre (ch. III) and the presence of fantastic elements (ch. IV). Here I would like to deal with the question of the differences between Seneca and his Roman predecessors. I will therefore attempt to analyse the general change in literary aesthetics which took place during Nero's reign and whose *spiritus movens* was Seneca himself. The second quotation at the beginning of this chapter is taken from Burke's treatise and will be very helpful in understanding Seneca's main aesthetic innovation.

As scholars have noted,[279] a very important feature of the style of Seneca's tragedies is its overwhelming massiveness — and this is particularly conspicuous in those

---

[277] J. Milton, *Paradise Lost* 2, 262-263.
[278] E. Burke, *op. cit.*, p. 157.
[279] *His style [...] does not attempt to reproduce the well proportioned grace and harmony of his "classical" predecessors, but creates its own heavier, "baroque" effects of overwhelming*

passages where he emulates his predecessors. While some classicists call Seneca's style "baroque",[280] others consider it to be "anticlassical"[281] and stress the fact that his tragedies depart from the tradition of classical drama. Be that as it may, scholars on the whole do appreciate Seneca's courage and his quest for literary freedom.[282]

Bold and decadent as it was, Seneca's style offended the taste of Roman grammarians and admirers of "Golden" Latin. Quintilian in particular disapproved of his innovations. This testimony is extremely important, as Quintilian belonged to the generation which came immediately after Seneca and must therefore have been very well acquainted with the literary taste of Seneca's times.[283]

Not only was Quintilian a witness to the changes in taste of Roman audiences, but he was also a literary connoisseur. As a teacher of Roman youth, he was the first to know about all the trends in literature and rhetoric — and one of these was "Senecanism", i.e. a tendency to imitate Seneca's style. These imitations were, however, often quite incompetent and in all probability that is what Quintilian had in mind when he wrote the following passage in his textbook:

Ex industria Senecam in omni genere eloquentiae distuli propter vulgatam falso de me opinionem, qua damnare eum et invisum quoque habere sum creditus. Quod accidit mihi, dum corruptum et omnibus vitiis fractum dicendi genus revocare ad severiora iudicia contendo. Tum autem solus hic fere in manibus adulescentium fuit. Quem non equidem omnino conabar excutere, sed potioribus praeferri non sinebam, quos ille non destiterat incessere, cum diversi sibi conscius generis placere se in dicendo posse, quibus illi placerent, diffideret. Amabant autem eum magis quam imitabantur, tantumque ab illo defluebant, quantum ille ab antiquis descenderat. Foret enim optandum, pares ac saltem proximos illi viro fieri. Sed placebat propter sola vitia et ad ea se quisque dirigebat effingenda, quae poterat; deinde cum se iactaret eodem modo dicere, Senecam infamabat. (Quint. *Inst.* 10, 1, 125-127)

It was no easy task to combat this fashion because Quintilian ran the risk of being accused by Seneca's young admirers of having a personal aversion towards Seneca, or — worse still, of being envious.[284] Quintilian explained that he merely

---

massivness, agitated and decentered movement, disorientating vastness, and emotional turbulence. (Ch. Segal, *Senecan Baroque...*, p. 325). Segal has shown that Seneca's versions are the highly original work of a powerful literary imagination.

[280] Cf. *ibidem*; cf. S. M. Goldberg, *Going for Baroque. Seneca and the English*, [in:] *Seneca in Performance*, pp. 209-231.

[281] Cf. A. Traina, *op. cit.*, pp. 10, 34, 93.

[282] *At times he deliberately disrupts the chains of school tradition: to him, the problem of "sublime" or "grand" style is not one of mere technique but one of the speaker's intellectual freedom.* (M. von Albrecht, *A History of Roman Literature*, vol. II, Leiden — New York — Köln 1997, p. 1186).

[283] Cf. J. Styka, *Estetyczne wartości literatury greckiej w krytycznym ujęciu M. F. Kwintyliana*, "Eos" 1980, 68, p. 325.

[284] *It would be unfair to accuse Quintillian of narrowness because his precepts for the student in the rhetorical school allow less scope for what we call originality. In the orator's world,*

disapproved of Seneca's faults (*vitia*) — which were, however, "sweet" (*dulcia*) enough to seduce the pretentious minds of young students.

On the other hand, we do not know exactly what Quintilian meant by the term *vitia*. His opinion that Seneca's imitators took only the worst things from him seems somewhat exaggerated. Quintilian's preference for Golden Latin is well known, so it seems quite natural that he simply could not accept an innovatory, non-classical style.

Another of Seneca's faults — according to Quintilian — was that his admirers preferred him to the whole pantheon of classical authors (*sed potioribus praeferri non sinebam*).[285] Quintilian simply could not accept the fact that such an innovatory and eccentric writer as Seneca was valued more than the icons of *Latinitas*. And to crown everything, there was the fact that Seneca himself had, on more than one occasion, criticized the *potiores* (*quos ille non destiterat incessere*). However — whether sincerely or merely to hide his true aversion to Seneca — Quintilian praises his numerous positive qualities. In the following sentence he expresses his disapproval of Seneca's idiosyncrasies:

> *Multae in eo claraeque sententiae, multa etiam morum gratia legenda; sed in eloquendo corrupta pleraque atque eo perniciosissima, quod abundant dulcibus vitiis. Velles eum suo ingenio dixisse, alieno iudicio. Nam si aliqua contempsisset, si parum non concupisset, si non omnia sua amasset, si rerum pondera minutissimis sententiis non fregisset, consensu potius eruditorum quam puerorum amore comprobaretur.* (Quint. *Inst.* 10, 1, 129-130)

Moreover, Quintilian openly accuses Seneca of corrupting the art of rhetoric (*in eloquendo corrupta pleraque*) and of some kind of literary ὕβρις (*si non omnia sua amasset*). On the other hand, in the *Epistulae morales* Seneca himself laments the falling standards of contemporary rhetoric:

> *Adice nunc, quod **oratio certam regulam non habet**: consuetudo illam civitatis, quae numquam in eodem diu stetit, versat. Multi ex alieno saeculo petunt verba, duodecim tabulas loquuntur. Gracchus illis et Crassus et Curio nimis culti et recentes sunt, ad Appium usque et Coruncanium redeunt. Quidam contra, dum nihil nisi tritum et usitatum volunt, in sordes incidunt. Utrumque diverso genere corruptum est, tam mehercules quam nolle nisi splendidis uti ac sonantibus et poeticis, necessaria atque in usu posita*

---

subject matter is imposed by practical relevance and governed by non-aesthetic limitations such as political expediency, or the definition of guilt under a given legal heading. There is little use for the originality of imagination which we praise so highly in works of poetry or fiction. (E. Fantham, *Imitation and Decline. Rhetorical Theory and Practice in the First Century after Christ*, "Classical Philology" 1978, 73, 2, p. 111).

[285] Quintilian recommended the *imitatio* of works by classical authors, who had achieved perfection of form: *Similem raro natura praestat, frequenter imitatio.* (Quint. *Inst.* 10, 2, 3). Cf. J. Styka, *Estetyczne wartości literatury greckiej...*, p. 326. Instead, his pupils followed the non-classical, extravagant style of Seneca, which Quintilian found absolutely unacceptable.

> *vitare. Tam hunc dicam peccare quam illum: alter se plus iusto colit, alter plus iusto neglegit; ille et crura, hic ne alas quidem vellit.* (*Epist.* 114, 13-14)

Seneca singles out two opposing groups of Latin orators whom he considers responsable for the decline of the art of rhetoric in Rome. He ridicules both the archaists, whose model was the law of the twelve tables (*duodecim tabulas loquuntur*),[286] and their opponents the Atticists, whose language was familiar and simple. He accuses both factions of lacking taste and moderation.

In these two extremes he sees the effects of a blind adherence to rules, whereas — in his opinion — speech had no strict rules (*oratio certam regulam non habet*) and should conform to the personality of the author and his individual nature, not some artificial principles.

He stuck to this opinion not only in his tragedies, but — above all — in the *Epistulae morales*.[287] The Latin of his day had already been corrupted by artificial trends and it was Seneca who — like Quintilian — defended it against blind imitation and exaggeration.[288] Indeed, he was the first Roman author to openly argue that an author's style must be a true reflection of his nature.[289]

Scholars see this sentence as being anticlassical[290] and have compared it with another place in the same letter 114, where Seneca confronts passive imitation with originality:

> *Quae apud Sallustium rara fuerunt, apud hunc crebra sunt et paene continua, nec sine causa: ille enim in haec incidebat, at hic illa quaerebat. Vides autem quid sequatur, ubi alicui vitium pro exemplo est. Dixit Sallustius: "aquis hiemantibus." Arruntius in primo libro belli Punici ait "repente hiemavit tempestas." Et alio loco cum dicere vellet frigidum annum fuisse, ait "totus hiemavit annus." Et alio loco: "inde sexaginta onerarias leves praeter militem et necessarios nautarum hiemante aquilone misit." Non desinit omnibus locis hoc verbum infulcire. Quodam loco dicit Sallustius: "dum inter arma civilia aequi bonique famas petit." Arruntius non temperavit, quo minus primo statim libro poneret ingentes esse "famas" de Regulo. Haec ergo et eiusmodi vitia, quae alicui inpressit imitatio, non sunt indicia luxuriae nec animi corrupti: propria enim esse debent et ex ipso nata, ex quibus tu aestimes alicuius adfectus: iracundi hominis iracunda oratio est, commoti nimis incitata, delicati tenera et fluxa.* (*Epist.* 114, 18-20).

For Seneca, the originality of an artist lies in his ability to create according to his own personality and not according to transitory fashions formed by an amor-

---

[286] Cf. A. Traina, *op. cit.*, p. 113.
[287] Cf. M. Wilson, *Seneca's Epistles to Lucilius. A Revaluation*, [in:] *Oxford Readings in Classical Studies*, ed. by J. G. Fitch, Oxford 2008, p. 83.
[288] Cf. G. M. A. Grube, *The Greek and Roman Critics*, London 1965, p. 269.
[289] Cf. M. Wilson, *Seneca's Epistles to Lucilius...*, pp. 82-83.
[290] Cf. G. M. A. Grube, *op. cit.*, p. 268.

phous multitude.²⁹¹ He can imitate, but according to his own taste, in the most natural way possible.²⁹² This is the clue which will allow us to understand his permanent rivalry with the Augustan poets. It will also enable us to explain the origins of his unique style.

If we understand all the hidden quotations from his predecessors as being sophisticated polemics with them, we will also be able to see the major aesthetic differences between Seneca and the models of his "active imitation" (the opposite of "passive imitation", which was something he detested).

In previous chapters I have used the term *aemulatio* in discussing hidden quotations in Seneca's tragedies. What we are dealing with, however, is not just rivalry, but also a literary technique which goes by the name of *referre idem aliter* — which is reminiscent of a more or less conscious discussion on literary taste.

This, of course, is merely a hypothesis, as Seneca might very well have incorporated whole passages of the works of other poets which were stored in his memory without even realizing it. Then he could simply have modified them according to the immanent laws of his "natural" style. This, however, is hardly likely, as we know that Roman intellectuals — and poets in particular — usually knew the works of Virgil and Ovid almost by heart. Seneca could not simply "borrow" a phrase and use it without remembering exactly who had written it and where.

If the borrowings were the result of an intentional strategy, this could only mean that Seneca had in all probability decided to emulate the classical masters. This would merely be the natural consequence of contemporary fashion, which actually obliged future poets to emulate those authors who had the best taste and style:

[...] ὡς καὶ ἄλλη τις παρὰ τὰ εἰρημένα ὁδὸς ἐπὶ τὰ ὑψηλὰ τείνει. ποία δὲ καὶ αὕτη; ἡ τῶν ἔμπροσθεν μεγάλων συγγραφέων καὶ ποιητῶν μίμησίς τε καὶ ζήλωσις. καί γε τούτου, φίλτατε, ἀπρὶξ ἐχώμεθα τοῦ σκοποῦ. (Pseud. Long. 13, 2)²⁹³

In the passage quoted above Pseudo-Longinus encourages his friend Postumius Terentianus to imitate great authors (μίμησις) and to emulate them (ζήλωσις).²⁹⁴ As

---

²⁹¹ Cf. *ibidem*, p. 269.
²⁹² Cf. *ibidem*.
²⁹³ Longinus is now considered by scholars to have lived more or less in Seneca's period: *This is* On the Sublime, *written in Greek by an unknown author referred to as Pseudo-Longinus. It was once thought that it had been written by a certain Dionysius Longinus who lived before Christ, but it is now believed that the author lived during the early part of the Christian period. His name is not known.* (J. J. Murphy, *The End of the Ancient World. The Second Sophistic and Saint Augustine*, [in:] *A Synoptic History of Classical Rhetoric*, Taylor & Francis e-Library 2008, p. 232). *Moreover, Seneca's style often borders on "the sublime", an ideal backed by the author of the* Περὶ ὕψους *("On the Sublime") who perhaps lived during the same epoch (cf.* epist. *41 on* animus magnus*).* (M. von Albrecht, *op. cit.*, pp. 1183-1184).
²⁹⁴ For Longinus μίμησις is not a pastiche, but a creative form of imitation (cf. Pseudo-Longinus, *op. cit.*, p. 113). *There is sometimes a difference between* μίμησις *and* ζῆλος: *Dion.*

the son of a teacher of rhetoric who grew up in the atmosphere of his father's school, Seneca excelled in all the techniques of *imitatio* and *emulatio*. It was therefore natural for him to maintain a sober and distant attitude towards the so-called canon of classical poetry. Indeed, he even dared to criticize what he disapproved of in the art of his models. This is what infuriated Gellius (Gell. *Noct. Att.* 12, 2) in Seneca's 22nd book of *Epistulae morales*, where he points out the faults of Cicero, Ennius and Virgil.

Although this book is lost, we have other passages, for example *Quaest. nat.* 3, 27, where Seneca criticises Ovid for having a style that is excessively light. In Seneca's times it was quite normal to look at the literary pantheon from a healthy distance in order to learn from them — as well as from their mistakes — rather than merely worship them.

Pseudo-Longinus himself draws attention to some of Homer's faults:

παρατεθειμένος δ'οὐκ ὀλίγα καὶ αὐτὸς ἁμαρτήματα καὶ Ὁμήρου καὶ τῶν ἄλλων ὅσοι μέγιστοι, καὶ ἥκιστα τοῖς πταίσμασι ἀρεσκόμενος, ὅμως δὲ οὐχ ἁμαρτήματα μᾶλλον αὐτὰ ἑκούσια καλῶν ἢ παροράματα δι' ἀμέλειαν εἰκῆ που καὶ ὡς ἔτυχεν ὑπὸ μεγαλοφυίας ἀνεπιστάτως παρενηνεγμένα, οὐδὲν ἧττον οἶμαι τὰς μείζονας ἀρετάς, εἰ καὶ μὴ ἐν πᾶσι διομαλίζοιεν, τὴν τοῦ πρωτείου ψῆφον μᾶλλον ἀεὶ φέρεσθαι, κἂν εἰ μηδενὸς ἑτέρου, τῆς μεγαλοφροσύνης αὐτῆς ἕνεκα. (Pseud. Long. 33, 4)

He is not as bold as Seneca, however, and claims that Homer's faults were not the result of negligence (οὐχ ... δι ἀμέλειαν), but were merely small imperfections[295] resulting from the magnanimity of the poet's nature (ὑπὸ μεγαλοφυίας), which was guilty of small lapses in the pursuit of great ideas.

Pseudo-Longinus was therefore a better diplomat than Seneca. He carefully avoided those forceful expressions which branded Seneca as an inveterate blasphemer in the eyes of conservative Roman critics.[296] Quintilian not only accuses him of having insufficient respect for the canon, but also suggests that Seneca was in love with his own ideas (*si non omnia sua amasset*).

Letter 114, however, says something which Quintilian probably did not understand or simply did not try to understand. What Seneca wishes to convey here is that

---

Hal. de imitatione, fr. 28 [...]. *This distinction, however, should not be read into passages where it is not expressed, and is certainly not relevant to L's point here. It is clear from the tenor of all this section that he places no value on mere pastiche, and is not talking about the mechanical reproduction of a model by rule.* (Ibidem).

[295] ὅμως δὲ ... παρενηνεγμένα: "deeming them nevertheless not so much voluntary mistakes as accidental slips let fall at random through inattention and with the negligence of genius". (*Ibidem*, p. 158).

[296] For Quintilian, the old Roman poets were sacred icons of higher art: *Ennium sicut sacros vetustate lucos adoremus* (Quint. *Inst.* 10, 1, 88). He saw nothing wrong in the fact that classical authors such as Cicero criticized other classical authors: *cum Ciceroni dormitare interim Demosthenes, Horatio vero etiam Homerus ipse videatur* (Quint. *Inst.* 10, 1, 25), but strongly disapproved of them being criticized by an innovatory writer such as Seneca, who himself was non-classical.

a writer should above all have a sound mind and be of good character, as only these can serve as guides towards achieving stylistic perfection:

> *Hoc a magno animi malo oritur: quomodo in vino non ante lingua titubat quam mens cessit oneri et inclinata vel prodita est: ita ista orationis quid aliud quam ebrietas nulli molesta est, nisi animus labat. Ideo ille curetur: ab illo sensus, ab illo verba exeunt, ab illo nobis est habitus, vultus, incessus. Illo sano ac valente oratio quoque robusta, fortis, virilis est: si ille procubuit, et cetera ruinam sequuntur. "Rege incolumi mens omnibus una est: amisso rupere fidem."* [Verg. Georg. IV, 212-213] *Rex noster est animus. Hoc incolumi cetera manent in officio, parent, obtemperant: cum ille paulum vacillavit, simul dubitant.* (*Epist.* 114, 22-23)

Quintilian for his part — in his *Institutio* — lists the rules which he considers to be mandatory for anyone aspiring to be a good writer.

In the same letter Seneca expresses his strong disapproval of the style of Maecenas and considers it to be a reflection of his bad morals:

> *Quomodo Maecenas vixerit notius est, quam ut narrari nunc debeat, quomodo ambulaverit, quam delicatus fuerit, quam cupierit videri, quam vitia sua latere noluerit. Quid ergo? Non oratio eius aeque soluta est quam ipse discinctus?* (*Epist.* 114, 4)

Seneca clearly does not do this out of rivalry or jealousy — he merely expresses his dislike of bad taste in a very blunt way. By contrast, when he criticizes Ovid — whom, as we have seen, he admires, but whose influence he also fears — he does so very subtly (e.g. *Quaest. nat.* 3, 27).

It seems that Seneca followed his own literary taste and also his own "nature" with great consistency, openly criticising the things which he did not like in the work of his literary predecessors, whilst at the same time developing his own innovatory style. This is probably what Quintilian was referring to when he complained of Seneca's arrogant attitude towards the classical poets and his excessive love of his own ideas.

As we have seen, Seneca was perfectly capable of criticizing both Maecenas, whom he considered the worst of poets, and Ovid, whom he considered the best. That criticism was not, as Quintilian suggested, the symptom of an inferiority complex with regard to other writers, but — on the contrary — the result of Seneca's individual judgment of their work and his personal disapproval of their aesthetic faults.

Quintilian was perfectly aware of Seneca's strong will (or perhaps stubbornness) as a stylist. That is probably why he writes: *quod voluit effecit* (Quint. *Inst.* 10, 1, 131) — which probably means that Seneca had fulfilled his deep yearning to create a new style and also a new aesthetic. This would seem to contradict Quintilian's former opinion that Seneca attacked his predecessors out of a frustrated longing for fame and appreciation.

Let us now look at what Quintilian wrote about Ennius, Cicero, Sallust, Virgil and Ovid — i.e. all those Roman authors with whom Seneca finds fault. He recommends that Ennius be venerated as a holy relic: *Ennium sicut sacros vetustate lucos adoremus* (Quint. *Inst.* 10, 1, 88) and compares Virgil to Homer: *ut apud illos Homerus, sic apud nos Vergilius auspicatissimum dederit exordium* (Quint. *Inst.* 10, 1, 85). As for Ovid, while he praises him alongside the other classical poets, he also chides him for the same reasons that he chides Seneca[297] — for having "too great a love of his own ideas" and for "(over-)indulgence" (*Ovidius et nimium amator ingenii sui, laudandus tamen partibus*, Quint. *Inst.* 10, 1, 88; *si ingenio suo imperare quam indulgere maluisset*, Quint. *Inst.* 10, 1, 98). By *indulgentia* he may mean both the eccentricity of Ovid's style and his bold choice of subjects (such as *Ars amatoria*).

Although he allowed writers to break the strict rules of style in certain cases (*expedit autem saepe mutare ex illo constituto traditoque ordine aliqua*, Quint. *Inst.* 2, 13, 8),[298] Quintilian also demanded that they respect such rules as *ordo* (Quint. *Inst.* 1, 10, 37), *dispositio* (Quint. *Inst.* 7, prooem. 22) and *compositio* (Quint. *Inst.* 9, 4, 116), which Seneca treated quite liberally.[299]

It therefore seems that both Ovid and Seneca were admonished by Quintilian for the same misdemeanours. Their common feature — a natural and innovatory style — was the reason why Seneca was so fascinated by Ovid. He had chosen him as the poet whose style and non-conformist taste best suited his own inclinations.

One very intriguing thing about Quintilian is that he never mentions Seneca's tragedies in the *Institutio oratoria*. Everything that he writes about Seneca refers to his style in general and he discusses only his philosophical works. In the same book, however, he writes at length about the tragedies of Varius, Ovid and Pomponius Secundus, Seneca's main rival:[300]

---

[297] *Quant à Sénèque, si Quintilien le condamne c'est par son voeu de «ramener à un goût (judicium) plus sévère notre façon d'écrire, corrompue par tant de défauts» ; car à l'instar d'Ovide, Sénèque laisse trop de liberté à son ingenium [...]. Ce dernier reproche — il est amoureux de sa propre écriture — vient se superposer, on le voit, à la formule que Quintilien employait plus haut pour exprimer le manque de jugement dont il cherchait à convaincre Ovide qui, lui aussi, aimait trop son propre génie (nimium amator ingenii sui).* (J. Brody, *Lectures Classiques*, Charlottesville 1996, p. 32).

[298] Cf. J. Styka, *Estetyczne wartości literatury greckiej...*, p. 307.

[299] This is the main difference between Quintilian's idea of originality and that of Seneca. While the former did not permit his pupils to break the rules of rhetoric, the latter was much more liberal. In Seneca's opinion it was the sober mind which guided the hand of the artist: *Rex noster est animus; hoc incolumi cetera manent in officio, parent, obtemperant* (*Epist.* 114, 23). According to Seneca, an author should be ashamed of ignorance, but never of his free will — and could even permit himself the luxury of making small grammatical mistakes: *Grammaticus non erubescet soloecismo si sciens fecit, erubescet si nesciens* (*Epist.* 95, 9).

[300] *Y aquí surge una cuestión difícil ¿por qué esta alabanza tan firme de un autor del que apenas conservamos una docena de versos, frente al olvidio de Séneca, de quien seguimos leyendo hoy nueve tragedias? No encontramos explicación para ello, si no es, claro está, el gran desinterés que muestra Quintiliano por la obra trágica del filósofo en el resto de la* Institutio.

Iam Varii Thyestes cuilibet Graecarum comparari potest. Ovidii Medea videtur mihi ostendere, quantum ille vir praestare potuerit, si ingenio suo imperare quam indulgere maluisset. Eorum quos viderim longe princeps Pomponius Secundus, quem senes [quidem] parum tragicum putabant, eruditione ac nitore praestare confitebantur. (Quint. *Inst.* 10, 1, 98)

There is a possible explanation for this inconsistency: Quintilian discusses Seneca "after all the genres of the art of eloquence" (*ex industria Senecam in omni genere eloquentiae distuli*, Quint. *Inst.* 10, 1, 125). He probably discusses his works as a whole, including the tragedies: *Tractavit etiam omnem fere studiorum materiam: nam et orationes eius et poemata et epistulae et dialogi feruntur* (Quint. *Inst.* 10, 1, 128-129). By *poemata* he probably means Seneca's tragedies.

Although Quintilian does not openly admit his dislike of Seneca's style (*propter vulgatam falso de me opinionem qua damnare eum et invisum quoque habere sum creditus*, Quint. *Inst.*10, 1, 125), this aversion can be detected in the manner in which he tries to do justice to his literary achievements. He declares: *multae in eo claraeque sententiae, multa etiam morum gratia legenda* (Quint. *Inst.* 10, 1, 129), but immediately adds: *sed in eloquendo corrupta pleraque, atque eo perniciosissima quod abundant dulcibus vitiis* (Quint. *Inst.* 10, 1, 129).

Seneca's main crime was that he ignored many classical rules of style which had been established and cherished by the *antiqui* (*defluebant quantum ille ab antiquis descenderat*, Quint. *Inst.* 10, 1, 126). His faults were *dulcia vitia*, "sweet faults"[301] because — as the *enfant terrible* of Roman literature — he had become the idol of young people thanks to his impassioned style and — in the opinion of Quintilian — was therefore a dangerous seducer of inexperienced minds. He was the kind of poet who attracted extravagant youth and appalled old, conservative scholars. The more conservative they were, the worse for Seneca:

De Annaeo Seneca partim existimant ut de scriptore minime utili, cuius libros adtingere nullum pretium operae sit, quod oratio eius vulgaria videatur et protrita, res atque sententiae aut inepto inanique impetu sint aut levi et causidicali argutia, eruditio autem vernacula et plebeia nihilque ex veterum scriptis habens neque gratiae neque dignitatis. Alii vero elegantiae quidem in verbis parum esse non infitias eunt, sed et rerum, quas dicat, scientiam doctrinamque ei non deesse dicunt et in vitiis morum obiurgandis severitatem gravitatemque non invenustam. (Gell. *Noct. Att.* 12, 2, 1)

(A. Pociña, *Quintiliano y el teatro latino*, "Cuadernos de Filología Clásica" 1981-1982, 17, pp. 99-100).

[301] *The chief exponent of the new style was Seneca. His language was characterized by antitheses, asymmetric puns, alliteration, paradoxes, unnatural expressions, aphorisms, a tendency to obscurantism, poetic flights of fancy. Quintillian thought his style totally corrupt, yet his success with the young, who tried hard to emulate his sweet vices (dulcia vitia) remained unequalled.* (E. Eyben, *Restless Youth in Ancient Rome*, London 1993, p. 151).

His worst enemies were the archaists. Quintilian's judgment is very mild compared with what Fronto writes about Seneca's style:[302]

Confusam eam ego eloquentiam, catachannae ritu, partim pineis nucibus Catonis, partim Senecae mollibus et febriculosis prunuleis insitam, subvertendam censeo radicitus, immo vero Plautinotato verbo, exradicitus. (Fronto, *De oration*. 1, 2)

Itane existimas graviores sententias et eadem e re apud Annaeum istum reperturum te quam apud Sergium? "Sed non modulatas aeque". Fateor. "Neque ita cordaces." Ita est. "Neque ita tinnulas." Non nego. Quid vero, si prandium idem utriusque apponatur, adpositas oleas alter digitis prendat, ad os adferat, ut manducandi ius fasque est, ita dentibus subiciat, alter autem oleas suas in altum iaciat, ore aperto excipiat, exceptas ut calculos praestrigiator primoribus labris ostentet? Ea re profecto pueri laudent, convivae delectentur; sed alter pudice pranderit, alter labellis gesticulatus erit. "At enim sunt quaedam in libris eius scite dicta, graviter quoque non nulla." Etiam lamminae interdum argentiolae cloacis inveniuntur; eane re cloacas purgandas redimemus? Primum in isto genere dicendi vitium turpissimum, quod eandem sententiam milliens alio atque alio amictu indutam referunt. (Fronto, *De oration*. 1, 3-5)

Not one to mince his words, Gellius calls Seneca a "stupid man" (*homo ineptus*):

Sed iam verborum Senecae piget; hac tamen inepti et insubidi hominis ioca non praeteribo: "quidam sunt" inquit "tam magni sensus Q. Ennii, ut, licet scripti sint inter hircosos, possint tamen inter unguentatos placere." (Gell. *Noct. Att.* 12, 2, 11)[303]

Let us now see what — apart from his style — could be non-classical or even anti-classical[304] in Seneca's work, for not only was he an innovator as regards Latin style, he was also very bold in choosing and presenting the subjects of his tragedies.

---

[302] Cf. C. J. T. Webb, *Fronto and Plutarch*, "The Classical Review" 1897, 11, 6, p. 306. *A sharp contrast between the stylistic austerity of Cato and the preciosity of Seneca is immediately obvious. It is also clear that even the harshness of Cato is preferable to the depraved ornament of Seneca, and that Fronto considers any attempt to fuse the two styles utterly impossible.* (C. Henderson, Jr., *Cato's Pine Cones and Seneca's Plums: Fronto p. 149 vdH*, "Transactions and Proceedings of the American Philological Association" 1955, 86, p. 257). *On the other hand stands Seneca with his mollibus et febriculosis prunuleis. The softness and cloying sweetness of an over-ripe plum is not a topic which requires scholarly exegesis, but we should attempt to determine to what, if to any, specific aspect of Senecan style the epithet mollis applies. Certainly it is in the strongest sense pejorative, and from this it is a reasonable guess that it may refer to composition, for it is in this area of criticism that mollis carries its strongest connotations of effeminacy. Seneca's depraved and jingling word arrangement is one of the dulcia vitia of which Quintilian speaks (Inst. 10.1.129), and it is probably to this that Fronto is referring when he castigates (149) sententiae eius tolutares, "his aphorisms that go trot, trot, trot." (Ibidem, pp. 260-261).*

[303] This is discussed further in: S. Hinds, *Allusion and Intertext: Dynamics of Appropriation in Roman Poetry*, Cambridge 1998, p. 72 ff.

[304] Cf. M. von Albrecht, *op. cit.*, p. 1183.

I have already mentioned his new approach to literary aesthetics, but I would now like to discuss this in the context of Seneca's conscious *aemulatio* of other poets, which resulted in some manifestations of his own artistic goals.

In the previous chapter I discussed the peculiar aesthetic of disgust, which is one of the most important features of Seneca's tragedies, and showed how disgusting things such as mutilated corpses were transformed into aesthetic objects. Ugliness in general is very important in Senecan tragedy. The characters are overcome by extreme passions and their states of mind are reflected by the physical appearance of the "represented world": the description of the grove in *Thyestes*, where a *locus terribilis* is the scene of a *scelus terribile*, is a very good illustration of this technique.

In earlier chapters I have compared passages from the *Metamorphoses* and the *Aeneid* with parallel passages from Senecan tragedies in order to analyse the literary techniques Seneca and his two predecessors used in order to achieve a similar effect. Now I would like to compare some passages from these works once again, but this time in order to see whether Seneca's *aemulatio* of Augustan poets was intentional or not.

The example I would like to discuss first of all is, of course, the scene of the feast in *Thyestes*, which is already famous for its intertextual links to Ovid's *Metamorphoses* and the narrative about Tereus.[305] Although scholars have already analysed these parallel passages very thoroughly,[306] it is worth taking a look at them once again just in order to examine Seneca's technique of *aemulatio*.

Before Seneca, the myth of Tereus had already been included in a tragedy about the Tantalids. I am referring, of course, to Aeschylus' *Agamemnon*, where the chorus alludes to the feast of Tereus (1140-1145). Perhaps Seneca associated the two myths directly, or perhaps it was a recent reading of the *Oresteia*[307] that inspired him to link the two myths and to emulate Ovid's version.

Let us take a look at the final passage of *Thyestes* — which in my opinion is the most significant intertextual passage of the play — and compare it with its Ovidian hypotext:

Ovid:
tantaque nox animi est: "<u>Ityn huc arcessite</u>" dixit.
Dissimulare nequit crudelia **gaudia** *Procne*
iamque suae cupiens exsistere nuntia cladis

---

[305] Cf. R. Jakobi, *op. cit.*, pp. 152-167; 204-205; cf. A. Schiesaro, *op. cit.*, pp. 70-138.

[306] *Ibidem.*

[307] Which is more probable, especially in view of the fact that both in Aeschylus and in Seneca Cassandra's function is similar: *Aeschylus' Cassandra is a brilliant substitute for a messenger. In her role as a seer she describes the regicide while it takes place (Schiller in Maria Stuart adapts the device), not afterwards, like the ordinary ἄγγελος. Seneca's Cassandra does this too (867-909), but survives to deliver the enigmatic last verse. Her death — like the death of Homer's Achilles — is not within the dramatic action.* (W. M. Calder III, Seneca's Agamemnon, "Classical Philology" 1976, 71, 1, p. 32).

"*intus habes, quem poscis*" *ait.* [...]
(Ovid. *Met.* 6, 652-655)

Seneca:
Thy. Satias dapis me nec minus Bacchi tenet.
Augere cumulus hic voluptatem potest,
*si cum meis **gaudere** felici datur.*
At. Hic esse natos crede in amplexu patris.
Hic sunt eruntque; nulla pars prolis tuae
tibi subtrahetur. Ora quae exoptas dabo
totumque turba iam sua implebo patrem.
(*Thy.* 973-979)

These passages show quite clearly the main aesthetic differences between Seneca and Ovid:

Ovid:
"*Ityn huc arcessite*" — "*intus habes, quem poscis*"

Seneca:
si cum meis gaudere felici datur — *Hic esse natos crede in amplexu patris*

The climax of *Thyestes* is therefore based on the climax of Ovid's narrative. Here we have its pattern:

1. Tereus / Thyestes want(s) to see his / their son / sons
2. Procne / Atreus replies that the boy(s) already is / are inside Thyestes' / Tereus' body.

The most common meaning of the verb *amplecti* is "to embrace". While Procne merely informs Tereus about what he has just done, Atreus is much more sophisticated: he reminds Thyestes that his sons are already held in his paternal embrace.[308] Unlike Tereus, who is quite direct, Atreus continuously plays with words[309] in order to torture Thyestes mentally.

Another interesting example of Seneca's technique within the same passage is line 994:

Ovid:
*Tantaque **nox** animi est.*
(Ovid. *Met.* 6, 652)

---

[308] *Atreus continues the grim parody of a happy reunion when he reassures an anxious Thyestes that he is already embracing his sons, who will never be parted from him* [...]. (G. Meltzer, *op. cit.*, p. 316).

[309] Cf. R. Jakobi, *op. cit.*, p. 166.

Seneca:

*caligo tenebris noxque se in **noctem** abdidit.*
(*Thy.* 994)

This passage was later imitated by Lucan:

*Nox subit atque oculos vastae obduxere **tenebrae**,
et miserum cernens agnoscere desinit Argum.*
(Luc. *Phars.* 3, 735-736)

Of course Seneca enlarges and exaggerates the effect, using two words which mean "darkness" (*caligo, tenebrae*) in the same line.[310] He also repeats the word "night" (*nox*) twice. Thyestes' momentary "mental eclipse" is followed by the eclipse of all the stars (*fugit omne sidus*, 995).

Exaggeration, exaggerated cruelty and the grotesque are also features of Ovid's narrative about Tereus.[311] Some parts of the *Metamorphoses*, such as the tale of Marsyas, could well have been inspired by contemporary Roman culture, especially by the amphitheatre, where people were mutilated by wild animals.[312]

Seneca highlights and magnifies the most expressive elements of Ovid's description of Tereus' feast. In addition, he juxtaposes the motif of a happy family (*si cum meis gaudere felici datur*, 975) with the actual misery of Thyestes, who has just eaten the bodies of his own children.

Ovid uses the verb *gaudia* to refer to Procne's triumph, while Seneca uses the same lexeme to refer to Thyestes, strengthening its expressive power further by using the adjective *felix*. He uses the same technique in line 977, where he repeats the verb *esse* and then juxtaposes its present and future forms (*hic sunt eruntque*).

Not only does Atreus tell Thyestes what has just happened — he also ironically adds that nobody could now tear the boys away from their father (*nulla pars prolis tuae / tibi subtrahetur*, 977-978). This expression appeals to the reader's imagination much more than Procne's words to Tereus: *intus habes quem poscis* (658).

Seneca tends to double and triple the effects achieved by Ovid, thus making his text more expressive. His nephew Lucan uses exactly the same technique. Let us look at three passages: from Ovid's tale of Tereus in the *Metamorphoses*, from Seneca's *Thyestes*[313] and from the scene of Pompey's death in Lucan's *Pharsalia*:

---

[310] This is a good example of Seneca's "effusiveness", which Mastronarde analyses on the example of *Oedipus*: [...] *the terms are naturally varied in a passage which exhibits a rhetorical fullness or effusion frequent in Senecan description.* (*op. cit.*, p. 344).

[311] Cf. K. Galinsky, *op. cit.*, p. 132.

[312] *Ibidem.*

[313] Jakobi has already analysed the first two passages as intertextually linked (cf. *op. cit.*, pp. 161-162). My intention here is merely to demonstrate how Seneca's technique worked and how well Lucan learnt it from his uncle.

Ovid:
ille indignantem et nomen patris usque vocantem
luctantemque loqui conprensam forcipe linguam
abstulit **ense** *fero; radix micat ultima linguae,*
ipsa iacet terraeque tremens **inmurmurat** *atrae,*
utque salire solet mutilatae cauda colubrae,
palpitat et moriens dominae vestigia quaerit.
Hoc quoque post facinus (vix ausim credere) fertur
saepe sua lacerum repetisse libidine corpus.
(Ovid. *Met.* 6, 555-562)

Seneca:
Nun. Stetit sui securus et non est preces
perire frustra passus; ast illi ferus
in vulnere **ensem** *abscondit et penitus premens*
iugulo manum commisit: educto stetit
ferro cadaver, cumque dubitasset diu
hac parte an illa caderet, in patruum cadit.
Tunc ille ad aras Plisthenem saevus trahit
adicitque fratri; colla percussa amputat;
cervice caesa truncus in pronum ruit,
querulum *cucurrit* **murmure incerto** *caput.*
(*Thy.* 720-729)

Lucan:
At postquam trunco cervix abscisa recessit,
vindicat hoc Pharius, dextra gestare, satelles.
Degener atque operae miles Romane secundae,
Pompei diro sacrum caput **ense** *recidis,*
ut non ipse feras? O summi fata pudoris!
Inpius ut Magnum nosset puer, illa verenda
regibus hirta coma et generosa fronte decora
caesaries conprensa manu est, Pharioque veruto,
dum vivunt voltus atque os in **murmura** *pulsant*
singultus animae, *dum lumina nuda rigescunt,*
suffixum caput est, quo numquam bella iubente
pax fuit; hoc leges Campumque et rostra mouebat,
hac facie, Fortuna, tibi, Romana, placebas.
(Luc. *Phars.* 8, 674-686)

Like Seneca, Lucan repeats a sequence of words derived from his hypotext:[314]

---

[314] Jamie Masters has made an excellent analysis of Lucan's emulation of Ovid (cf. *op. cit.*, p. 59 ff.). As we can see above, Lucan uses exactly the same technique of emulation as Seneca does.

Ovid:
***ense** — <u>fero</u> — **inmurmurat** — <u>lacerum</u>*

Seneca:
*<u>ferus</u> — **ensem** — <u>truncus</u> — **querulum** — **murmure incerto***[315] *— <u>caput</u>*

Lucan:
*<u>trunco</u> — **ense** — <u>feras</u> — **murmura** — **singultus animae** — <u>caput</u>*

Seneca chose some words from his hypotext and repeated them in the parallel passage of his own work, which later became Lucan's hypotext.[316]

The most gruesome deed Tereus commits is to repeatedly rape the mutilated Philomela (*saepe sua lacerum repetisse libidine corpus*, Ovid. *Met.* 6, 562), while Atreus brutally murders three people in rapid succession in the same scene. Whereas Ovid tries to soften the effect with the comment *vix ausim credere* (Ovid. *Met.* 6, 561),[317] Seneca lays additional stress on the very action of killing (*in vulnere ensem abscondit, et penitus premens / iugulo manum commisit*, *Thy.* 722-723; *colla percussa amputat*, *Thy.* 727; *ac pueri statim / pectore receptus ensis in tergo exstitit*, *Thy.* 740-741), prolonging the naturalistic descriptions.

The sons of Thyestes meet their deaths in a spectacular way, like gladiators in an amphitheatre. The moment of death of the first of Thyestes' sons is revealed in slow motion (*educto stetit / ferro cadaver*, *Thy.* 723-724). While Philomela's tongue — cut out by Tereus — mutters some words on the ground, the head of Tantalus — Thyestes' second son — is described as *querulum*, which means "groaning" and its muttering is *incertum* — "unclear".

This analysis shows how Seneca changes his hypotext in order to achieve something quite different. He overcomes the fear of remaining under Ovid's spell by intensifying the power of the words with which he builds his poetry. He gives the greatest achievements of Latin literature a new face, in accordance with his own literary "manifesto".

---

[315] Jakobi would seem to have been the first to notice this borrowing (cf. *op. cit.*, pp. 161--162).

[316] Martha Malamud has noticed Lucan's dependence on Ovid, but not on Seneca, who was — as our analysis has shown — his primary hypotext: *Just as Pompey's final moments saw him imitating a number of different exemplars, so his head recalls other exemplary severed heads. Vergil had cast his Priam in the image of the dead Pompey, breaking the illusion of realism in his description of the sack of Priam's palace to describe the king, slain at the altar inside the house, as a headless corpse lying on the shore: iacet ingens litore truncus / avolsumque umeris caput et sine nomine corpus (Aen. 2.557-58). Ovid, imitating this passage in his parody of epic battles, describes another old man, Emathion, brutally slain at an altar; his head bounces on the altar, its tongue still cursing, and breathes its last amid the flames (Met. 5.104-6).* (cf. *Pompey's Head and Cato's Snakes*, "Classical Philology" 2003, 98, 1, pp. 35-36).

[317] Seneca alludes to these words in the chorus: *credat hoc quisquam?* (*Thy.* 456).

Scholars have found a passage in the *Epistulae morales* where Seneca advises his friend Lucilius to be fearless of established tradition in taking up famous themes:[318]

Multum interest, utrum ad consumptam materiam an ad subactam accedas: crescit in dies et inventuris inventa non obstant. Praeterea condicio optima est ultimi: parata verba invenit, quae aliter instructa novam faciem habent. Nec illis manus inicit tamquam alienis. Sunt enim publica. [Iurisconsulti negant quicquam publicum usu capi.]. Aut ego te non novi aut Aetna tibi salivam movet. Iam cupis grande aliquid et par prioribus scribere. Plus enim sperare modestia tibi tua non permittit, quae tanta in te est, ut videaris mihi retracturus ingenii tui vires, si vincendi periculum sit: tanta tibi priorum reverentia est. (Epist. 79, 6-7)

This is exactly what Seneca does.[319] He faces up to his famous predecessors and rivals by taking up the subjects of their poems, by indirectly addressing them (e.g. by means of verbal sequences or allusions) and rewriting their poems in the spirit of a new aesthetic of his own.

Scholars have noted that Seneca not only achieves visual effects, but also plays with the sounds of the Latin language. For example, in lines 728-729 he accumulates the sound "k / q" (repeated 9 times) and "u" (repeated 11 times).[320] Lines 728-729 also abound in so-called *littera canina*, i.e. the letter "r", which the Romans found rather annoying:

cervice caesa truncus in pronum ruit,
querulum cucurrit murmure incerto caput.
(*Thy.* 728-729)

There is another interesting aesthetic difference between the passage from Ovid's tale of Tereus and the final part of Seneca's *Thyestes* discussed above: while the narrator in the *Metamorphoses* maintains a certain distance from the terrible events he is relating, the envoy in *Thyestes* is very excited by his story and the chorus is only too eager to hear it.

---

[318] Cf. A. Schiesaro, *op. cit.*, p. 52.

[319] *Seneca's tragedies stem from a continuous, even obsessive confrontation with their models […]. The pervasive characteristic of Seneca's tragedies is their belatedness: they represent an anachronistic return to the past, a frustrated desire for lost forms mediated by an overwhelming and oppressive intertextual memory.* (*Ibidem*, p. 223).

[320] Cf. R. J. Tarrant, *op. cit.*, p. 194. As Ingarden argues, the level of sounds is normally kept to an absolute minimum in the process of "concretization". However, there may be cases where sounds play an important part, depending on the way a literary work is composed, and also on the reader's type of imagination (he may find a special aesthetic pleasure in sounds, cf. *Szkice z filozofii literatury*, p. 86). In Ingarden's terminology "concretization" means the filling in by the reader's or listener's imagination of the "partially undetermined places" (*miejsca niedookreślenia*) in the structure of a work of literature (cf. idem *The Literary Work of Art*, p. 246 (§ 38 in chapter VII); cf. W. Iser, *op. cit.*, p. 170 ff.).

Whereas the Ovidian narrator is very cautious and tries to soften the horrors of his account by the use of similes and certain rhetorical devices (e.g. he tells the reader that he too is frightened by what he is saying), the envoy in *Thyestes* gives his account slowly and in such a manner that the members of the chorus become impatient to know the details of the murder committed by Atreus (*Quid deinde* [...] *facit? / Puerone parcit, an scelus sceleri ingerit?*, *Thy*. 730-731).[321] He lets the dreadful details be known one at a time, depicting them in a very naturalistic way.

Where Ovid carefully avoids an accumulation of horrors, Seneca actively pursues it. This is the most significant feature of his cruel Muse, which is so different from the subtle Muses of Ovid and Virgil. Seneca gives us a comprehensive account of the terrible events around which the plots of his plays revolve.

Another difference between Seneca and the Augustan poets is the fact that where Ovid and Virgil show only one gruesome episode, Seneca — as we have seen in *Thyestes* — knows no limits at all. Let us compare a short summary of Ovid's tale of Tereus and a similar summary of Seneca's *Thyestes:*

Ovid:
Procne and Tereus marry.
Tereus travels to Athens.
Tereus mutilates and rapes Philomela.
Tereus comes back to Thrace.
Procne mourns Philomela.
Procne discovers the truth.
Procne finds Philomela.
Procne and Philomela kill Itys.
The preparation of the feast (short).
The feast (short).
The recognition (short).
Procne, Philomela and Tereus turn into birds.

Seneca:
Tantalus infects the palace with evil.
Atreus plans his vengeance on Thyestes.
Thyestes arrives at the palace with his sons.
The description of a locus terribilis.
Atreus prepares the sacrifice — the prodigia.
Atreus murders the sons of Thyestes (long).
Atreus prepares the meal from their bodies (long).
Thyestes has his supper (long).
The recognition (long).
Atreus mocks Thyestes.

From these summaries, the main difference between Ovid's tale and Seneca's tragedy is quite clear. Ovid does not avoid cruelty and the macabre. On the contrary

---

[321] Cf. R. Jakobi, *op. cit.*, p. 162.

— he is fascinated by the weird and wild Greek myths. For example, he does not hesitate to describe the lingering death of Marsyas in a very naturalistic way:[322]

Clamanti cutis est summos direpta per artus,
nec quicquam nisi vulnus erat; cruor undique manat,
detectique patent nervi, trepidaeque sine ulla
pelle micant venae; salientia viscera possis
et perlucentes numerare in pectore fibras.
(Ovid. *Met.* 6, 387-391)

The description, however, is short. Ovid is still very careful about using his aesthetic discovery and tries not to overdo horrifying scenes — and in particular avoids bringing them together. He prefers to make them as short as possible, so that they practically merge into one episode.

By contrast, Seneca tends to overwhelm his audience with a series of macabre scenes, often choosing the most horrible one to be the climax of the whole play. For example, the climax of *Thyestes* is the ἀναγνώρισις — the moment when Atreus shows Thyestes the heads of his sons. That scene is not related by an envoy — as it should be according to the laws of classical drama — but is shown in full *hic et nunc*.

Of course, in the case of the *Metamorphoses*, Ovid enjoyed a greater liberty of composition, while in the case of *Thyestes* the order of events was dictated by the structure of the tragedy.[323] Be that as it may, Seneca was free not to show so many gory details and not to prolong the macabre descriptions.

Thyestes is undoubtedly the only Senecan tragedy which — at no risk of over-interpretation — we may consider to be his aesthetic manifesto. Let us examine the passage where Seneca consciously alludes to Ovid:

At. Nescioquid animus maius et solito amplius
supraque fines moris humani tumet
instatque pigris manibus — haud quid scit scio,
sed grande quiddam est. Ita sit. **Hoc, anime, occupa**
(dignum est Thyeste facinus et dignum Atreo,
quod uterque faciat): vidit infandas domus
Odrysia *mensas — fateor, immane est scelus,*
sed occupatum: maius hoc aliquid dolor
inveniat. **Animum Daulis inspira parens**

---

[322] The description of Marsyas' death is very compact, however. *But Ovid hardly offers us a set-piece of Grand Guignol, and indeed the story receives highly concentrated treatment in only nineteen lines.* (Ch. Martindale, *Redeeming the Text...*, p. 63).

[323] *Even a play such as "Thyestes", which testifies to the degree of originality and freedom that the poet enjoys in the treatment of his chosen theme, cannot escape a largely predeterminated series of events.* (A. Schiesaro, *op. cit.*, pp. 222-223).

sororque; causa est similis: assiste et manum
impelle nostram. Liberos avidus pater
gaudensque laceret et suos artus edat.
Bene est, abunde est: hic placet poenae modus
tantisper. Ubinam est? Tam diu cur innocens
servatur Atreus? **Tota iam ante oculos meos**
imago caedis errat, *ingesta orbitas*
in ora patris — anime, quid rursus times
et ante rem subsidis? Audendum est, age:
quod est in isto scelere praecipuum nefas,
hoc ipse faciet. […]
(Thy. 267-286)

This is the most metaliterary passage of the entire play. Inspired by the myth of Tereus (*animum Daulis inspira parens/ sororque*, 275-276),[324] Atreus expresses an ardent wish to outdo Procne's crime. Moreover, he desires to commit a crime that would exceed the bounds of human decency (*supra fines moris humani*, 268). He wishes to "occupy" a new idea (*sed grande quiddam est. Ita sit. Hoc, anime, occupa*, 270) which would assure him the title of *the* original criminal — and he is worried that the "slot" of the ideal crime may already have been "occupied" or taken by someone else (*immane est scelus, / sed occupatum*, 273-274).

Atreus here may be the *porte-parole* of Seneca himself. He expresses a passionate desire to commit a crime that nobody has ever committed before. If we substitute "Seneca" for "Atreus" and the word "artefact"[325] for "crime" (*nefas*), we can see that this passage may actually be a hidden confession of the poet's anxiety to be original,[326] as well as of his strong will to outdo the predecessor with whom he is so obsessed.[327] Atreus-Seneca obviously does not like the fact that the wonderful idea has already been taken or "occupied" by someone else,[328] so he

---

[324] *Subsequently, as the* satelles *is reduced to a completely impotent sparring partner, who does little more than feed his master the next line, Atreus caps his own poetic prologue by describing in further detail the grandiose* nefas *he is plotting, and by invoking his own special Muses, Procne and Philomela (267-277).* (Ibidem, p. 52).

[325] *His "nefas", as we will see, is an eloquent poetic artefact, a deceitful ploy whose author ("quid sit quod horres et auctorem indica", says the chorus at line 369: "tell what it is that makes you shudder, and point out its author") fully exploits the potential of words to ensnare and betray. Atreus' "nefas" is the core of action of the whole tragedy, the well-devised and well-acted scheme to which Thyestes is doomed to succumb.* (Ibidem, p. 50).

[326] Cf. Ch. Segal, *Language and Desire in Seneca's "Phaedra"*, Princeton 1986, p. 298; cf. A. Schiesaro, *op. cit.*, p. 221.

[327] *If all post-Ovidian literature is programatically self-conscious to a very high degree, Seneca's own narcissism takes the form of a sustained critique of authorial responsibility as it is showcased in the author's staged counterparts — a group of obsessed, determined criminals.* (A. Schiesaro, *op. cit.*, p. 224).

[328] Schiesaro has also pointed out that Seneca may be emulating not only Ovid, but also earlier Roman tragedians: *While Seneca ostensibly espouses an alternative version of the mythical*

takes it upon himself to show that — at the very least — he can do a far better job than Procne-Ovid.[329]

Read as Seneca's confession of his intertextual strategy,[330] the passage quoted above would seem to reveal his real attitude towards Ovid, whom he considers to be both his master and his rival. Atreus' words also betray Seneca's quest for originality and his dread of mere imitation. Just as Atreus cannot content himself with imitating Procne, so Seneca cannot content himself with merely imitating Ovid — he must do better.[331]

When Atreus at last discovers that he really can surpass Procne, he expresses his satisfaction with the words: *bene est, abunde est: hic placet poenae modus/ tantisper* (279-280). The plan is really very simple: instead of only one child (Procne killed her only son, Itys), he undertakes to kill all three sons of Thyestes. In our intertextual "translation" this means that Seneca undertakes to compose an even more macabre work than Ovid ever did.

Whereas the Ovidian narrator expresses his horror of Tereus' deed — and communicates his healthy distance from the contents of his narrative to the listener with the words: *vix ausim credere* (Ovid. *Met.* 6, 561) — the Senecan villain encourages his own mind not to hesitate to commit the most ghastly crime of all time with the words: *anime, quid rursus times / et ante rem subsidis? audendum est, age* (vv. 283-284).[332]

If this interpretation of the two lines is correct, it would seem that Atreus' monologue is indeed Seneca's reply to Ovid — and, indeed, a manifesto of his own literary aesthetic. Moreover, it conforms to the expressive and anticlassical aesthetic of Seneca's tragedies, which do not shun the macabre and the shocking.

However bold and revolutionary Ovid may seem, he still belongs to the Augustan generation of poets who worshipped classical beauty. It was Seneca who definitely abandoned the classical ideals and opened up a new period in the history of Roman literature. Not only did he abandon the traditional *decorum*, but — in

---

plot and makes Thyestes' return contingent on Atreus' deceitful invitation, he transforms Accius' (and presumably Varius') version into a powerful subplot which substantially affects our perception of the events. (Ibidem, p. 142).

[329] *These features — in particular the programmatic combination of novelty and awareness of the tradition — would be enough to lend Atreus' declaration of intents a distinct literary colour, even if he had not used a number of key terms which Seneca elsewhere applies explicitly to poetic creation. (Ibidem, pp. 52-53).*

[330] *I owe the term intertextual strategy to Schiesaro (cf. ibidem, p. 81).*

[331] *Seneca competes with his model at a metanarrative level as well, further blurring the distinction, already problematic in Ovid, between good and evil. Atreus' desire to surpass all previous horrors powerfully reflects the play's agonistic relationship with its literary ancestor. (Ibidem, p. 78); Thyestes invokes an epic text as its authorizing Muse, and as a fundamental model that must not only be equaled, but surpassed. (Ibidem, p. 83).*

[332] *Atreus has read his Ovid, and displays through a number of revealing allusions a detailed knowledge of Tereus' story, in particular of Procne's avenging plans. (Ibidem, p. 77).*

a flagrant breach of the division of the genres³³³ — he also chose to use epic poetry as the foundation for his dramatic style.

The blurring of the borders of the genres is one of the symptoms of anticlassicism. The process of the "declassicization"³³⁴ of Roman poetry began with Ovid, who treated the genres rather liberally,³³⁵ e.g. writing an epic poem in elegiac metre. Seneca went further, finding that epic techniques were much more useful than their dramatic counterparts (e.g. *locus horridus*, the preponderance of narrative over dialogue, detailed descriptions, the quoting of one character by others etc.).

It was Ovid, therefore, who pioneered the change of aesthetics in Roman literature. He was the first to exploit negative aesthetic qualities and the first to introduce macabre motifs into his works (such as Tereus' feast). We may say that he was the first Roman poet to experiment with literature and to challenge traditional taste. This was why Seneca chose Ovid as his master and rival and why critics such as Quintilian criticized him for being a conceited "genius".

The Augustan period was undoubtedly a classical age.³³⁶ Ovid was the youngest poet of his generation and his aesthetic was already somewhat different. This is why some scholars consider him to be a "baroque" poet.³³⁷ His art mirrors the shift from Augustan times to the "Neronian baroque".³³⁸

The general taste of Seneca's times was not classicist in the least. Along with political insecurity and oppression, the period of mad emperors brought a fascination with negative aesthetic qualities — the grotesque, the weird, the shocking and even the disgusting.³³⁹ The classical ideals of harmony and beauty no longer suited these turbulent times.³⁴⁰

Seneca's plays may therefore be seen as a *signum temporis* of the aesthetic and also the political changes which took place during his lifetime, reflecting as they do the general atmosphere of Nero's Rome. The characters of these tragedies are

---

[333] *Generic affiliations become all the more pertinent when Ovid himself steps into the picture so that simple labels such as "epic" (or indeed "tragic") cease to be encompassing or definitive. (Ibidem, p. 83).*

[334] According to Wallis' theory, some historical periods (e.g. the 5th-4th centuries B.C. in Greece, the Renaissance and Classicism in the 18th-19th centuries A.D.) are particularly fond of harmony and beauty. These are the classicist periods, as opposed to the baroque (e.g. the Hellenistic period, the Baroque, or modern times) which prefer disharmony and disfigurement (cf. *op. cit.*, pp. 25, 200).

[335] Cf. A. Schiesaro, *op. cit.*, p. 83.

[336] I mean the classicist aesthetics which became *an official artistic programme* in Augustan Rome. Cf. H. Peyre, *op. cit.*, pp. 209-214; cf. M. Torelli, *Roman Art, 43 B.C.-A.D. 69*, [in:] *The Cambridge Ancient History*, vol. X: *The Augustan Empire, 43 B.C.-A.D. 69*, ed. by A. K. Bowman, E. Champlin, A. Lintott, Cambridge 1996, p. 930.

[337] Cf. C. Segal, *Senecan Baroque...*

[338] Cf. M. von Albrecht, *op. cit.*, p. 1072.

[339] In accordance with the theory of aesthetic cycles, Seneca's times were a baroque period (cf. M. Wallis, *op. cit.*, p. 105).

[340] Cf. *ibidem*, p. 106.

hysterical and obsessive,[341] just like Tiberius, Caligula, Nero and many of Seneca's closest contemporaries.

It was Ovid who actually discovered the great potential of negative aesthetic qualities, though he used them sparingly — only when and where it was absolutely essential. Unlike Seneca, who exploited them to the full, Ovid treated them as a colourful addition to the whole of his poetic.[342]

Seneca was not content to be Ovid's imitator — or even his successor. He achieved originality by dint of the fact that he constructed his literary aesthetic on the new foundation of negative aesthetic qualities — disharmony, the macabre and the sublime[343] — abandoning once and for all the traditional Horatian canon of classical *decorum*.

---

[341] Cf. A. Schiesaro, *op. cit.*, p. 224. *Overwhelmed by emotions beyond his control, the Senecan tragic hero becomes alienated from an aspect of his own humanity, from the rational moderation of desire, hatred, love, fear, hope, despair, and guilt. No wonder our own age of decentred emotionality has rediscovered these works.* (Ch. Segal, *Boundary Violation and the Landscape of the Self in Senecan Tragedy*, [in:] *Oxford Readings... Seneca*, p. 140).

[342] As he was still bound by the rules of Augustan classicism.

[343] Of course, in the Burkean sense (cf. E. Burke, *op. cit.*).

Conclusion

In this book I have set myself the task of analysing the aesthetics of Senecan tragedy. In order to do this, I have had to discuss their affinity with the epic genre, given that Seneca might not have chosen other tragedies as his models, but rather epic poems — and in particular Virgil's *Aeneid* and Ovid's *Metamorphoses*, the latter being the main object of his *aemulatio*.

I have tried to show that Seneca uses many literary techniques which are typical of epic poetry. These techniques often take precedence over dramatic techniques and at times are even used as substitutes for them. As a result, description often plays a greater role than dialogue.

Seneca's extensive use of epic strategies pushed his tragedies in the direction of epic poetry. Their actual purpose — if we accept the hypothesis that they were not intended to be staged — is therefore very similar to that of epic poetry. They appeal to the audience with the directness of drama (there being no omniscient narrator), but by means of narrative and description.

Senecan tragedies are therefore dramatic in form and epic in purpose. As a result, the principal means by which they reach their audience is not direct on-stage presentation, but a verbal account. The characters act both as *dramatis personae* and as individual, epic narrators.

This is why Seneca paid so much attention to vocabulary, choosing words whose meanings were particularly intense and colourful. He did so in order to make his descriptions more expressive, so that they could appeal all the more easily to the listener's imagination.

Seneca elaborated a special technique — which I have called the "contrast technique" — by means of which he constructed powerful verbal images. This proved particularly useful in *Thyestes*, where in the same descriptions Seneca juxtaposed opposing elements such as day and night, life and death, and beauty and ugliness.

In each such pair of contrasting ideas, the negative element invariably defeats and destroys its opposite. The vision of the world which Seneca presents to his audience in these tragedies is very fatalistic. His "represented world" gradually degenerates into a cataclysm. The mechanism of the "contrast method" mirrors the mechanism of the events in the plays, where good succumbs to evil.

Seneca's tragedies are highly expressive not only as regards their style, but also as regards the construction of the "represented world", in whose centre Seneca places death and the disfigurement of the human body. His tragedies, especially *Thyestes*, abound in correspondingly lugubrious descriptions.

Seneca maintained his plays in a new, expressionist aesthetic which was constructed on a foundation that was quite different from that of the Augustan period. Unlike the Augustan poets, Seneca preferred negative aesthetic qualities, which in his tragedies prevail over the positive.

The "sharp" aesthetic of these plays, with its gruesome and macabre descriptions, does have a reason. Like the contrast technique, it too reflects the laws which rule the "represented world" of Senecan tragedy. Physical destruction and the disfigurement of the human body serve to illustrate the moral decline of the characters.

The great potential of negative aesthetic qualities had already been discovered by Ovid, who was the last of the Augustans and the harbinger of new taste in literature. He was, however, still fettered by the rules of traditional, classicist aesthetics and did not exploit his discovery to the full. This allowed Seneca — who had long been fascinated by the *Metamorphoses* — to seize the opportunity to become an original poet. He founded the aesthetic of his tragedies on what was a marginal (albeit very important) facet of the aesthetic of Ovid.

Bibiliography

A. Critical Editions, Commentaries and Translations

- Aristoteles, *De arte poetica liber*, ed. by W. Christ, Leipzig 1910.
- Cicero M. T., *"Academicorum" reliquiae cum "Lucullo"*, ed. by O. Plasberg, Leipzig 1932.
- Cicero M. T., *Ad M. Brutum Orator*, ed. by W. Friedrich, Leipzig 1909.
- Cicero M. T., *De divinatione, De fato, Timaeus*, ed. by R. Giomini, Leipzig 1914.
- Cicero M. T., *De natura deorum*, ed. by O. Plasberg, Leipzig 1917.
- Cicero M. T., *Epistulae ad familiares*, ed. by D. R. Shackleton Bailey, Cambridge 1977, vol. I-II.
- Diogenes Laertios, *Vitae philosophorum*, ed. by H. S. Long, Oxford 1964.
- Fronto M. C., *M. Cornelii Frontonis et M. Aurelii imperatoris epistulae*, ed. by A. Naber, Lipsiae 1867.
- Gellius A., *Noctes Atticae*, ed. by P. K. Marshall, Oxford 1968.
- Horatius Q., *Opera*, ed. by S. Borzsák, Leipzig 1984.
- Lucanus M. A., *Belli Civilis libri decem*, ed. by K. Hosius, Leipzig 1913.
- Lycophronus, *Alessandra*, ed. with an introd., transl. and comm. by V. Gigante Lanzara, Milano 2000.
- Ovidius P., *Le Metamorfosi*, introd. by G. Rosati, transl. by G. F. Villa, Milano 2005.
- Ovidius P., *Tristium libri V, Ibis, Ex Ponto libri IV*, ed. by R. Ehwald, F. Waltharius Levy, Leipzig 1922.
- Plinius C. C., *Epistularum libri novem, Epistularum ad Traianum liber, Panegyricus*, ed. by C. F. W. Mueller, Leipzig 1903.
- Pseudo-Longinus, *On the Sublime*, ed. with a comm. by D. A. Russell, Oxford 1964.
- Quintilianus C. F., *Institutio oratoria*, ed. by L. Radermacher, Berlin 1971, vol. I-II.
- *Remains of Old Latin*, ed. by E. H. Warmington, vol. I-II, London 1956-1957.
- Seneca L. A., *Ad Lucilium epistulae morales*, ed. by L. D. Reynolds, vol. I-II, Oxford 1991.
- Seneca L. A., *Agamemnon*, ed. with a comm. by R. J. Tarrant, Cambridge 1976.
- Seneca L. A., *De beneficiis libri VII, De clementia libri II*, ed. by K. Hosius, Leipzig 1914.
- Seneca L. A., *I dialoghi*, vol. I: *Della provvidenza, Della constanza del saggio, Dell'ira*, ed. by G. Viansino, Milano 1992.
- Seneca L. A., *I dialoghi*, vol. II: *Consolazione a Marcia, Della vita felice, Della vita appartata, Della tranquillità dell'animo, Della brevità della vita, Consolazione a Polibio, Consolazione a Elvia*, ed. by G. Viansino, Milano 2000.

- Seneca L. A., *Medea*, transl. with an introd. by F. Ahl, New York 1986.
- Seneca L. A., *Medea*, ed. with a comm. by C. D. N. Costa, Oxford 1989.
- Seneca L. A., *Naturalium Quaestionum libri VIII*, ed. by A. Gercke, Leipzig 1986.
- Seneca L. A., *Phaedra*, ed. with a comm. by R. Mayer, M. Coffey, Cambridge 1990.
- Seneca L. A., *Phoenissae*, introd. and comm. by M. Frank, Leiden 1995.
- Seneca L. A., *Thyestes*, with a comm. by R. J. Tarrant, Atlanta 1985.
- Seneca L. A., *Tragedies I: Hercules Furens, Troades, Phoenissae, Medea, Phaedra*, ed. and transl. by J. G. Fitch, Harvard 2002.
- Seneca L. A., *Tragedies II: Oedipus. Agamemnon. Thyestes. Hercules in Oeta. Octavia*, ed. and transl. by J. G. Fitch, Harvard 2002.
- Seneca L. A., *Tragoediae*, ed. by O. Zwierlein, Oxford 1986.
- Seneca L. A., *Troades. A Literary Introduction with Text, Translation and Commentary*, ed. with an introd., transl. and comm. by E. Fantham, Princeton 1982.
- Seneca L. A., *Tutte le tragedie*, ed. and transl. by E. Paratore, Roma 2004.
- Seneca Maior L. A., *Controversiae*, ed. by A. Kiessling, Lepizig 1872.
- Suetonius C., *Vitae Caesarum*, transl. by J. C. Rolfe, introd. by K. R. Bradley, vol. I-II, Cambridge 2001.
- Vergilius P., *Eneide*, introd. and comm. by E. Paratore, transl. by L. Canali, Milano 2006.
- Vergilius P., *Georgiche*, transl. by A. Barchiesi, ed. by A. Barchiesi, G. Biagio Conte, Milano 1989.

B. Studies in Seneca and Roman Tragedy

- Albrecht M. von, *A History of Roman Literature*, vol. II, Leiden — New York — Köln 1997.
- Bishop J. D., *Seneca's Daggered Stylus. Political Code in the Tragedies*, Meisenheim am Glan 1985.
- Boyle A. J., *Tragic Seneca. An Essay in the Theatrical Tradition*, London 1997.
- Braginton M., *The Supernatural in Seneca's Tragedies*, Menasha 1933.
- Calder W. M. III, *Originality in Seneca's Troades*, "Classical Philology" 1970, 65, 2, pp. 75-82.
- Calder W. M. III, *Seneca's Agamemnon*, "Classical Philology" 1976, 71, 1, pp. 27-36.
- Calder W. M. III, *Theatrokratia. Collected Papers on the Politics and Staging of Greco--Roman Tragedy*, ed. by S. Smith, Zürich — New York 2005.
- Erasmo M., *Roman Tragedy. Theatre to Theatricality*, Austin 2004.
- Fantham E., *Virgil's Dido and Seneca's Tragic Heroines*, "Greece & Rome", Second Series, 1975, 22, 1, pp. 1-10.
- Ferrin Sutton D., *Seneca on the Stage*, Leiden 1986.
- Fitch J., *Playing Seneca?*, [in:] *Seneca in Performance*, ed. by W. M. Harrison, London 2000, pp. 1-12.
- Friedrich W. H., *Die Raserei des "Hercules"* (1967), [in:] *Senecas Tragödien*, ed. by E. Lefèvre, Darmstadt 1972, pp. 131-148.
- Goldberg S. M., *Going for Baroque: Seneca and the English*, [in:] *Seneca in performance*, ed. by G. W. M. Harrison, London 2000, pp. 209-231.
- Harrison G. W. M., *"Semper ego auditor tantum?". Performance and physical setting of Seneca's plays*, [in:] *Seneca in Performance*, ed. by G. W. M. Harrison, London 2000, pp. 137-149.

- Henderson Ch., Jr., *Cato's Pine Cones and Seneca's Plums: Fronto p. 149 vdH*, "Transactions and Proceedings of the American Philological Association" 1955, 86, pp. 256-267.
- Henry D., Walker B., *Phantasmagoria and Idyll. An Element of Seneca's "Phaedra"*, "Greece & Rome", Second Series, 1966, 13, 2, pp. 223-239.
- Hermann L., *Le Théatre de Sénèque*, Paris 1924.
- Hine H., *Interpretatio Stoica of Senecan Tragedy*, [in:] *Sénèque le tragique*, ed. by M. Billerbeck, E. Schmidt, Genève 2004, pp. 173-209.
- Hook B. S., *Nothing within which passeth show. Character and "color" in Senecan Tragedy*, [in:] *Seneca in Performance*, ed. by G. W. M. Harrison, London 2000, pp. 53-71.
- Jakobi R., *Der Einfluß Ovids auf den Tragiker Seneca*, Berlin 1988.
- Jamróz W., *Herakles i Dejanira Seneki jako exempla*, "Meander" 1972, 27, pp. 64-79.
- King Ch. M., *Seneca's "Hercules Oetaeus". A Stoic Interpretation of the Greek Myth*, "Greece & Rome", Second Series, 1971, 18, 2, pp. 215-222.
- Knoche U., *Eine Brucke vom Philosophen Seneca zum Tragiker Seneca* (1941), [in:] *Senecas Tragodien*, ed. by E. Lefèvre, Darmstadt 1972, pp. 58-66.
- Knoche U., *Senecas Atreus. Ein Beispiel* (1941), [in:] *Senecas Tragödien*, ed. by E. Lefèvre, Darmstadt 1972, pp. 477-489.
- Kocur M., *We władzy teatru*, Wrocław 2005.
- Lefèvre E., *"Quid ratio possit?". Senecas Phaedra als stoisches Drama* (1969), [in:] *Senecas Tragödien*, ed. by E. Lefèvre, Darmstadt 1972, pp. 343-375.
- Lefèvre E., *Schicksal und Selbstverschuldung in Senecas Agamemnon* (1966), [in:] *Senecas Tragödien*, ed. by E. Lefèvre, Darmstadt 1972, pp. 457-476.
- Leo F., *De Senecae tragoediis observationes criticae*, Berlin 1879.
- Liebermann W. L., *Senecas Tragödien. Forschungsüberblick und Methodik*, [in:] *Sénèque le tragique*, ed. by M. Billerbeck, E. Schmidt, Genève 2004, pp. 1-48.
- Littlewood C., *Self-Representation and Illusion in Senecan Tragedy*, Oxford 2004.
- Malaspina E., *Pensiero politico ed esperienza storica nelle tragedie di Seneca*, [in:] *Sénèque le tragique*, ed. by M. Billerbeck, E. Schmidt, Genève 2004, pp. 267-307.
- Mantovanelli P., *El Hado, la casualidad, el reino (Notas a Sen. "Oed." 22 sigs., 980 sigs.; "Thy." 604 sigs., 32 sig.; "Oed." 882 sigs.)*, [in:] *Seneca. Dos mil años después. Actas del Congreso Internacional de su Nacimiento*, ed. by M. Rodríguez-Pantoja Márquez, Cordoba 1997, pp. 237-244.
- Mantovanelli P., *Il prologo del "Tieste" di Seneca. Strutture spazio-temporali e intertestualità*, "Quaderni di Cultura e di Tradizione Classica" 1992, 10, pp. 201-216.
- Mantovanelli P., *Le menadi immemori (Sen. Oed. 440 ff.). Sulle funzioni di un coro Senecano*, [in:] *Nove studi sui cori tragici di Seneca*, ed. by L. Castagna, Milano 1996, pp. 105-123.
- Mantovanelli P., *Lo strappo lungamente atteso. Il caso di Sen. "Oed." 961*, "Quaderni di Cultura e di Tradizione Classica" 1994, 12, pp. 89-97.
- Mantovanelli P., *"Populus infernae Stygis". Il motivo dei dannati del mito in Seneca tragico*, "Quaderni di Cultura e di Tradizione Classica" 1993, 11, pp. 135-147.
- Marti B., *Seneca's Tragedies. A New Interpretation*, "Transactions and Proceedings of the American Philological Association" 1945, 76, pp. 216-245.
- Marti B., *The Prototypes of Seneca's Tragedies*, "Classical Philology" 1947, 42, 1, pp. 1-16.
- Marshall C. W., *Location! Location! Location! Choral absence and theatrical space in "Troades"*, [in:] *Seneca in Performance*, ed. by G. W. M. Harrison, London 2000, pp. 27-51.

- Mastronarde D., *Seneca's "Oedipus". The Drama in the Word*, "Transactions and Proceedings of the American Philological Association" 1970, 101, pp. 291-31.
- Mayer R., *Seneca: "Phaedra"*, London 2002.
- Meltzer G., *Dark Wit and Black Humor in Seneca's "Thyestes"*, "Transactions of the American Philological Association" 1988, 118, pp. 309- 330.
- Miola R. S., *Shakespeare and Classical Tragedy. The Influence of Seneca*, Oxford 1992.
- Motto A. L., Clark J. R., *Senecan Tragedy*, Amsterdam 1988.
- Nisbet R. G. M., *The Dating of Seneca's Tragedies, with Special Reference to "Thyestes"*, [in:] *Oxford Readings in Classical Studies. Seneca*, ed. by J. G. Fitch, Oxford 2008, pp. 348-371
- Owen W., *Commonplace and Dramatic Symbol in Seneca's Tragedies*, "Transactions and Proceedings of the American Philological Association" 1968,99, pp. 291-313.
- Paratore E., *Der "Hercules Oetaeus" stammt von Seneca ist fruher als der "Furens"* (1958), [in:] *Senecas Tragödien*, ed. by E. Lefèvre, Darmstadt 1972, pp. 545-558.
- Park Poe J., *An Analysis of Seneca's Thyestes*, "Transactions and Proceedings of the American Philological Association" 1969, 100, pp. 355-376.
- Pease S., *On the Authenticity of the Hercules Oetaeus*, "Transactions and Proceedings of the American Philological Association" 1918, 49, pp. 3-26.
- Pociña A., *Quintiliano y el teatro latino*, "Cuadernos de Filología Clásica" 1981-1982, 17, pp. 97-110.
- Pratt N. T., Jr., *Dramatic Suspense in Seneca and his Greek Precursors*, Princeton 1939.
- Pratt N. T., Jr., *Seneca's Drama*, Chapel Hill 1983.
- Przychocki G., *Styl tragedyj Anneusza Seneki*, Kraków 1946.
- Pypłacz J. *"Gotyckie" elementy w tragediach Seneki*, "Symbolae Philologorum Posnaniensium Graecae et Latinae" 2008, XVIII, pp. 273-285.
- Pypłacz J., *The Terrible and the Sublime. Some Notes on Seneca's Poetics*, "Classica Cracoviensia" 2007, XI, pp. 289-301.
- Regenbogen O., *Schmerz und Tod in den Tragödien Senecas*, [in:] *Vorträge 1927-1928 zur Geschichte des Dramas*, ed. by F. Sachsl, Berlin 1930, pp. 167-218.
- Rosenmeyer T., *Senecan Drama and Stoic Cosmology*, Berkeley 1989.
- Rostropowicz J., *Władysława Strzeleckiego uwagi o aluzjach politycznych w niektórych tragediach Seneki*, [in:] *Mistrz Władysław Strzelecki (1905-1967)*, ed. by L. Stankiewicz, Wrocław 2006, pp. 97-102.
- Schiesaro A., *The Passions in Play. "Thyestes" and the Dynamics of Senecan Drama*, Cambridge 2003.
- Schmidt E. A., *Zeit und Raum in Senecas Tragödien. Ein Beitrag zu seiner dramatischen Technik*, [in:] *Sénèque le tragique*, ed. by M. Billerbeck, E. Schmidt, Genève 2004, pp. 321-356.
- Segal Ch., *Boundary Violation and the Landscape of the Self in Senecan Tragedy*, [in:] *Oxford Readings in Classical Studies. Seneca*, ed. by J. Fitch, Oxford 2008, pp. 136-156.
- Segal Ch., *Language and Desire in Seneca's "Phaedra"*, Princeton 1986.
- Segal Ch., *Senecan Baroque. The Death of Hippolytus in Seneca, Ovid and Euripides*, "Transactions of the American Philological Association" 1984, 114, pp. 311-325.
- Shelton J., *The spectacle of death in Seneca's "Troades"*, [in:] *Seneca in Performance*, ed. by G. W. M. Harrison, London 2000, pp. 87-118.
- Smereka J., *De Senecae tragoediis dinosis colore fucatis*, "Eos" 1929, 32, pp. 615-650.

- Stamm R., *The Mirror-Technique in Senecan and Pre-Shakespearean Tragedy*, Bern 1975.
- Tarrant R. J., *Greek and Roman in Seneca's Tragedies*, "Harvard Studies in Classical Philology" 1995, 97 (*Greece in Rome: Influence, Integration, Resistance*), pp. 215-230.
- Tarrant R. J., *Senecan Drama and its Antecedents*, "Harvard Studies in Classical Philology" 82, 1978, pp. 213-263.
- Tietze Larson V., *The Role of Description in Senecan Tragedy*, Frankfurt am Main 1994.
- Traina A., *Lo stile "drammatico" del Filosofo Seneca*, Bologna 1978.
- Varner E. R., *Grotesque vision. Seneca's tragedies and Neronian art*, [in:] *Seneca in Performance*, ed. by G. W. M. Harrison, London 2000, pp. 119-136.
- Wesołowska E., *Postaci w "Medei" i "Fedrze" Seneki*, Poznań 1991.
- Wesołowska E., *Prologi tragedii Seneki w świetle komunikacji literackiej*, Poznań 1998.
- Wesołowska E., *Seneka w oczach Władysława Strzeleckiego. Kilka uwag*, [in:] *Mistrz Władysław Strzelecki (1905-1967)*, ed. by L. Stankiewicz, Wrocław 2006, pp. 73-79.
- Wesołowska E., *Seneki i Marka Aureliusza ars moriendi*, "Studia Classica et Neolatina" 1998, 3, pp. 169-197.
- Wilson M. *Seneca's Epistles to Lucilius. A Revaluation*, [in:] *Oxford Readings in Classical Studies*, ed. by J. G. Fitch, Oxford 2008, pp. 59-83.
- Wilson M., *The Rhetoric of the Younger Seneca*, [in:] *A Companion to Roman Rhetoric*, ed. by W. Dominik, J. Hall, Malden—Oxford—Victoria 2007, pp. 425-438.
- Zapata Ferrer M. de la Almudena, *"Descriptiones" en las tragedias de Séneca*, "Cuadernos de Filología Clásica" 1988, 21, pp. 373-380.
- Zwierlein O., *Die Rezitationsdramen Senecas*, Meisenheim am Glan 1966.

C. Other Studies

- Auguet R., *Cruelty and Civilization. The Roman Games*, London 1994.
- Barchiesi A., *The Crossing*, [in:] *Texts, Ideas and the Classics. Scholarship, Theory, and Classicsl Literature*, ed. by S. J. Harrison, Oxford 2001, pp. 140-163.
- Barrett J., *Staged Narrative. Poetics and the Messenger in Greek Tragedy*, Berkeley 2002.
- Beacham R. C., *Spectacle Entertainments of Early Imperial Rome*, Yale 1999.
- Biagio Conte G. *Latin Literature. A History*, Baltimore 1994.
- Biagio Conte G., *The Rhetoric of Imitation. Genre and Poetic Memory in Virgil and Other Latin Poets*, transl. by Ch. Segal, New York 1986.
- Bieber M., *The History of the Greek and Roman Theater*, Princeton 1961.
- Bloom H., *The Anxiety of Influence. A Theory of Poetry*, New York 1973.
- Booth W. C., *The Rhetoric of Fiction*, Chicago 1961.
- Bogumił I., *Adaptacje sceniczne czy dramaty? Antyczny epos jako źródło łacińskich tragedii i tragikomedii przełomu XVI i XVII wieku*, Gdańsk 2007.
- Boyle A. J., *The Canonic Text: Virgil's Aeneid*, [in:] *Roman Epic*, ed. by idem, London 1993, pp. 79-107.
- Brody J., *Lectures Classiques*, Charlottesville 1996.
- Burke E., *A Philosophical Enquiry into the Sublime and Beautiful*, ed by D. Womersley, London 2004.

- Danielewicz J., *Technika opisów w "Metamorfozach" Owidiusza*, Poznań 1971.
- Eco U., *Historia brzydoty*, a collective translation, Poznań 2007.
- Eco U., *Historia piękna*, tansl. by A. Kuciak, Poznań 2005.
- Eco U., *The Open Work*, transl. by A. Cancogni, introd. by D. Robey, Cambridge (Mass.) 1989.
- Eco U., *The Role of the Reader. Explorations in the Semiotics of Texts*, Bloomington 1984.
- Eyben E., *Restless Youth in Ancient Rome*, London 1993.
- Fantham E., *Imitation and Decline. Rhetorical Theory and Practice in the First Century after Christ*, "Classical Philology" 1978, 73, 2, pp. 102-116.
- Fantham E., *Ovid's "Metamorphoses"*, Oxford 2004.
- Fantham E., *Roman Literary Culture From Cicero to Apuleius*, London 1999.
- Frye N., *Anatomy of Criticism. Four Essays*, Princeton 1971.
- Frye N., *Collected Works on Renaissance Literature*, ed. by M. Dolzani, Toronto 2006.
- Frye N., *Fearful Symmetry*, Princeton 1969.
- Futrell A., *Blood in the Arena. The Spectacle of Roman Power*, Texas 1997.
- Futrell A., *The Roman Games*, Padstow 2006.
- Galinsky G. K., *Ovid's "Metamorphoses". An Introduction to the Basic Aspects*, Oxford 1975.
- Gibson B., *Ovid on Reading: Reading Ovid. Reception in Ovid*, Tristia 2, [in:] *Oxford Readings in Classical Studies*, ed. by A. Laird, Oxford 2006, pp. 346-379.
- Grube G. M. A., *The Greek and Roman Critics*, London 1965.
- Hardie P., *Virgil and Tragedy*, [in:] *The Cambridge Companion to Virgil*, ed. by Ch. Martindale, pp. 312-326.
- Harris M. S., *Two Postulates of Expressionism*, "The Journal of Philosophy" 1929, 26, 8, pp. 210-215.
- Hinds S., *Allusion and Intertext. Dynamics of Appropriation in Roman Poetry*, Cambridge 1998.
- Ingarden R., *Das literarische Kunstwerk*, Halle 1931.
- Ingarden R., *O dziele literackim*, transl. by M. Turowicz, Warszawa 1960.
- Ingarden R., *Szkice z filozofii literatury*, introd. by W. Stróżewski, Kraków 2000.
- Ingarden R. *The Literary Work of Art*, transl. by G. G. Grabowicz, Evanston 1979.
- Ingarden R., *Wybór pism estetycznych*, ed. with an introd. by A. Tyszczyk, Kraków 2005.
- Iser W., *The Act of Reading. A Theory of Aesthetic Response*, Baltimore 1981.
- Jantzen G. M., *Death and the Displacement of Beauty*, London 2004.
- Kyle D. G., *Spectacles of Death in Ancient Rome*, London 1998.
- Le Bon G., *The Crowd. A Study of the Popular Mind*, Dover 2002.
- Leigh M., *Lucan. Spectacle and Engagement*, Oxford 1997.
- Macksey R., *Longinus Reconsidered*, "Modern Language Notes" 1993, 108, 5, Comparative Literature, pp. 913-934.
- Malamud M., *Pompey's Head and Cato's Snakes*, "Classical Philology" 2003, 98, 1, pp. 31-44.
- Mantovanelli P., *Perchè Ovidio non si poteva fermare (Sen. Rhet. Contr. 9, 5, 17)*, "Classica Cracoviensia" 2000, 5, pp. 259-273.
- Martindale Ch., *Latin Poetry and the Judgement of Taste. An Essay in Aesthetics*, Oxford — New York 2005.
- Martindale Ch., *Redeeming the Text. Latin Poetry and the Hermeneutics of Reception*, Cambridge 1993.

- Masters J., *Poetry and Civil War in Lucan's "Bellum Civile"*, Cambridge 1992.
- Milton J., *Paradise Lost*, ed. by D. Bush, Oxford 1966.
- Murphy J. J., *The End of the Ancient World. The Second Sophostic and Saint Augustine* (1972), [in:] *A Synoptic History of Classical Rhetoric*, Taylor & Francis e-Library 2008, pp. 127-150.
- Otis B., *Ovid As an Epic Poet*, Cambridge 1966.
- Peyre H., *Co to jest klasycyzm?*, transl. by M. Żurowski, Warszawa 1985.
- Pianezzola E., *Ovidio. Modelli retorici e forma narrativa*, Bologna 1999.
- Plass P., *The Game of Death in Ancient Rome. Arena Sport and Political Suicide*, London 1995.
- Solmsen F., *The World of the Dead in Book 6 of the "Aeneid"*, [in:] *Oxford Readings in Vergil's "Aeneid"*, ed. by J. Harrison, Oxford 1990, pp. 208-223.
- Stabryła S., *Latin Tragedy in Virgil's Poetry*, Wrocław 1970.
- Styka J., *Estetyczne wartości literatury greckiej w krytycznym ujęciu M. F. Kwintyliana*, "Eos" 1980, 68, pp. 303-327.
- Styka J., *Estetyka stosowności (decorum) w literaturze rzymskiej*, Kraków 1997.
- Styka J., *La littérature grecque à la lumière de l'appréciation esthétique des auteurs romains depuis Auguste jusqu'au IIe siècle après J.-Ch.*, transl. by B. Hrehorowicz, Wrocław 1987.
- Tatarkiewicz W., *Estetyka starożytna*, Wrocław 1962.
- Torelli M., *Roman Art, 43 B.C.-A.D. 69*, [in:] *The Cambridge Ancient History*, vol. X: *The Augustan Empire, 43 B.C.-A.D. 69*, ed. by A. K. Bowman, E. Champlin, A. Lintott, Cambridge 1996, pp. 930-958.
- Wallis M., *Wybór pism estetycznych*, ed. with an introd. by T. Pękala, Kraków 2004.
- Wikarjakówna T., *Rola zwiastuna w tragedii greckiej*, "Symbolae Philologorum Posnaniensium" 1979, IV, pp. 3-39.